OUT OF
DARKNESS
INTO
MARVELOUS
LIGHT

OUT OF
DARKNESS
INTO
MARVELOUS
LIGHT

Berniece Bernay (BB)

OUT OF DARKNESS INTO MARVELOUS LIGHT

iUniverse books may be ordered through booksellers or by contacting:

iUniverse
1663 Liberty Drive
Bloomington, IN 47403
www.iuniverse.com
1-800-Authors (1-800-288-4677)

ISBN: 978-1-5320-0106-2 (sc)
ISBN: 978-1-5320-0107-9 (e)

Library of Congress Control Number: 2016910399

Print information available on the last page.

iUniverse rev. date: 06/24/2016

Contents

INTRODUCTION

Not by might, nor by power, but by my spirit, saith the Lord of hosts. Zechariah 4:6.

This introductory scripture indicates that whatsoever you face in life, you need this same power of God.

We all have some misfortune chapters in our lives therefore, this book is designed to open the eyes of everyone who is suffering in or from bad situations and do not know which way to turn or go. BB just want to say that storms are often broadcast in everyone's life. One is either in a storm already or heading into one, either way, stormy weather I in everyone' forecast.

i   The life of Bernice Bernay.

Berniece Bernay, better known to family and friends as BB was born in a little town called Quaint Paradise on November 18th 1947. She is the second of ten siblings. At the age of six she started the Robinson Elementary School. The town is so small that it only has one Elementary school. While she was there, she won many spelling Bee contests and always was at the top of her class. BB was never given the opportunity of attending a secondary school since it wasn't any established on her little island but she still dreamt of furthering her education one day to become a writer or a star dancing and acting in the big world before millions of people.

ii   What life meant for BB.

Life for BB meant, family, friends who she can trust and they in turn can trust her. Her educational career was teaching. Her hobbies were reading, writing acting followed by a happy marriage and at least two beautiful children a son and a daughter. It was all about the things she likes and do not like. The community in which she lived, the happy and sad moments of disappointing and unfortunate episodes that took place in her life from childhood to adult.

In BB's conclusion, she had encountered many obstacles and road blocks. Her life was like a roller coaster with its attached carts filled not with people but problems such as loneliness, abandonment, troubles, trials and injustices. Therefore, in writing this book it is my prayer and aim that it will be an inspiration and an apparatus to help you find a happy, satisfying, free and worthwhile life. It is written for the sole purpose of encouraging abused victims to stand on the promises of God that will transform their life. If you want to know more of BB's life. Continue reading the story.

DEDICATION

This Book is dedicated to the family, friends of the author and to all the hurting and abused women across the world.

ACKNOWLEDGEMENTS

Berniece Bernay, affectionately known as BB will like to thank the Holy Spirit who has given her the inspiration and drive to write a book of this nature.

Many thanks go to her family and friends who have encouraged her to write this inspiring book and to all who have contributed in some way or the other thus, enabling the author to cry out to God and to reach out to the many hurting women out there. Thank you God for placing them into her pathway.

Thanks to the persons who encouraged BB to make this publication a reality. Without you, the message sent forth would not be made possible and successful. To all, her hat, she tipped for assisting her with her healing process.

To the evaluator, editor and publisher for their part in the development in completing this production of this proclamation. For this BB is very grateful. Thank you!

Finally, thanks to all the readers. BB feels a deep sense of satisfaction and gratitude.

OUT OF DARKNESS INTO MARVELOUS LIGHT

By Berniece Bernay (BB)

CHAPTER 1

A DISTURBED CHILDHOOD

"You made all the delicate, inner parts of my body and knitted me together in my mother's womb. Thank You for making me so wonderfully complex. Your workmanship is marvelous - and how well I know it. You watched me as I was being formed in utter seclusion as I was woven together in the dark of the womb. You saw me before I was born. (Psalms 139:13–16 NLT).

Berniece Bernay's birth at first, was described by her parents at first as being healthy and perfect. Within months, they discovered a scar surfacing on the left side of her face. It looked almost the shape of a triangular. This however, led to deep concern. Back then, there were no state – of – the art medical facilities and no trained doctors stationed on the island. Since it is only a tiny golden link connected to a chain of islands, it was difficult to accommodate such a scar.

Babies then, were delivered by experienced house nurses called midwives. They continued to monitor her condition to see if it was an acne that will just fade away or a physical defect that will leave her scarred for life. As she matured, the scar became more and more visible. This did not bother BB during her toddler age but as soon as she developed the ability to recognize who she really was, the mirror mischievously made her conscious of the blemish.

The time soon came for her debut at school, she looked and felt different, inferior, shy and afraid. Unanswered questions began to flood her mind as to what am I going to do? Is she going to have any friends? Will her classmates love or play with her as she was? What will the other boys and girls think of her? Are they going to tease or make fun of her? In a spilt second it came to her that she was only a child who will notice or who will care? Everything went well for about two years. BB played, laughed and joked together until she forgot her defect. This lasted only throughout her kindergarten years.

As BB watched herself crossed over from that phase of life to the primary level, things began to changed. Her feathers began dropping out one by one and so did her friends. They soon began to notice her physical make-up. Suddenly, making fun of her became their specialty. They began to see her as the 'Ugly Duckling so to speak. Within seconds, she became withdrawn and frightened, too frighten to go to school. She felt all alone.

This harassment continued day after day. Often times her older sister will get into little spats for her. She was and still is very bold and brave and not afraid of anyone. It was not because of what she had told her but by what she saw and heard from her peers. This made BB very sad because she was never a warrior so she felt like a coward.

Someone may ask, where were her parents in all of this? She couldn't tell them what was going on for fear they would not believe her. So she kept it all hidden inside. Even though she was constantly bullied, it did not hinder her performance in class.

She refused to let it. BB, always put up a brave front in class but whenever she gets home in the quiet of the night, she would cry herself to sleep dreading the next school day.

Days, weeks, months and years passed, the gang continue their provoking and aggravating insults and being made fun of daily. One day, BB decide she could not bear it any longer and vowed that she would fight back but in a flash, she knew that was not what God wanted for her. Whilst on her mission, a stabbing feeling arose in her chest followed by a faint tormenting voice saying, No! No! No! my child don't do it; it isn't worth it. BB looked around in shock but saw no one. The voice was so strong in her head she had no choice but to obey. She withstood it all.

During recess time, sitting all alone, BB began to asked herself, why was she being treated that way. What has she done to be treated like a nobody at school and then at home where no one seemed to care. Home yes home! A place where love and communication were absent. Judging from the actions of her parents, she sensed that their life was not a bed of roses therefore, making it difficult for them to sit and communicate with her. Within that period, her father travelled a lot to foreign countries to seek employment to support his family thus leaving her mother all alone to take care of a large family in the home.

Growing older, gave her the quest for knowledge. She became curious about her ancestors (a topic never touched). BB began to probed into the past history to find out who they were, their traits, their culture, their names. What were they like? Were they rich or poor? Is she anything like them? She knew only of her mother's parents and from an expression frequently used by her grandmother quite often when in anger was, "Don't make my African blood rise indicated that she was of an African descent.

Another thing BB remembered about her grandmother was that she was a very difficult person to get along with but underneath that umbrella of toughness and unusual disposition, there was still some compassion and love hidden inside especially for her grandchildren. As for her father, she is still baffled as to who his relatives really were and are and where they came from.

BB's deceased grandfather – her father's father was the only Bernay in the island. After her father died, she became curious as to who her grandfather was, where he came from and who was his family. That was a subject her father never talked about except that his mother was married twice. She never knew or met any of her deceased father's family. Watching her father daily, she got the impression that he himself did not know much about his family. BB confessed that up to this date, she still does not know who her relatives really are on her father's side.

Both of BB's parents were very strict or should she say too strict. They were very religious. That was what she loved, admired and appreciated the most about them raising her. They made sure that as a family she was in Sunday School and Church every Sunday, rain, blow or sunshine the family had to be there. They also made sure that the family prayed individually every night before going to bed.

Throughout the facet of BB's childhood life, she could only recall and talk about these happy moments. On Christmas Eve, when her mother will give her three shillings (British Currency were used then) to go shopping. Back then, she thought she was rich very rich (smile). On Christmas Day, she would allow her to visit relatives and they in turn would spend a few hours over at her house. As a family, we were not allowed to have friends. Another happy moment was when her father would gather the family around the table and relate old Anancy stories and other tales which made her laugh. He always made the family laugh at his jokes. He had a sense of humor.

BB always looked forward to the arrival of Christmas. That special day meant a toy, new clothing and lots of delicious food of all kinds and types. The house always took on a festive atmosphere. Hours if not days were spent baking cakes and brewing wine from sea grapes and ripe pears from the cactus plant. BB would assist with the decorations for the home, giving it a new facelift by painting it with white wash which was a type of homemade pure white limestone made from burnt conch shells and heavy logs of wood.

In the meantime, BB family continued to grow from one to ten, six boys and four girls thus, creating a lot of mouths to feed. During this time, things began to worsen. It became very rough and tough for the family. Hard times crept in. Her father than made a decision to travel abroad to seek a livelihood for the family. After staying away for a number of years, he returned becoming Jack and master of all trades. During his tenure abroad he left mother as the disciplinarian of the family. To BB the tactics used were very severe.

Back then, BB thought it was the worse type of discipline ever. After becoming an adult, she saw that the harshness was stemmed from frustration and hard times. Her thoughts began to race. She always dreamt of a home as being a safe haven where there is freedom, love, contentment, protection and well-nurtured, sometimes a hug or a kiss. She felt confused terming her life as a 'Disturbed Childhood'. Life was unfair to her even in the place she called home.

BB's greatest cravings of security were knowing that someone really and truly cared for her by spending precious teachable moments with her. She felt like something was missing from her life. To BB it seems as if her parents had forgotten the Word that says "teach your children to choose the right path and when they are older, they will remain upon it."

After experiencing these unfortunate circumstances, her admonition to parents using the words of St. Paul in his writing in Ephesians 6:4 (TLB) "Do not keep on scolding and nagging your children, making them angry and resentful. Rather, bring them up with loving discipline the Lord Himself approves, with suggestions and godly advice."

Solomon also wrote in Proverbs 13:24 (NLT): "Make sure discipline your children in the correct way. If you love them, you will be prompt to discipline them in the right way. Give them the love and affection at home and you will prevent them from desiring to go and find it in the world. Love no matter what shape or form they are in, or even how they look or speak. Make them know that their body is the temple of the Lord and God loves them just the way they are. If you love them, you will see good results. Lead by example teach them not only by your words but also by your actions."

Hug and kiss your children. Reach beyond the limitations and communicate with them. Read God's Word and pray with them, for a family that prays together stays together.

BB concluded this chapter by saying, parents, your meaningful relationship and companionship with your children, will cause them to see and appreciate your wise counsel and will discover the joys of living on the promises of God's Word that will forever bless them. God place a high priority on family throughout life. The fifth commandment echoed children would learn to honor, respect and obey when they see you the parents honoring one another. Most importantly, when they observe your obedience and faithfulness to the Almighty God. Finally, give your children the love, time and attention, for it is a gift that doesn't come easily and cheaply. These were her missed opportunities of a "Disturbed Childhood".

CHAPTER 2

BLIND CONTRAVENTION

Don't let anyone think less of you because you are young. (1Timothy 4:12).

BB's schooling era came to an end at the age of thirteen. It was a period in her life that marked the beginning of reality. This transition came with strange unfamiliar feelings developing in her, both physically and emotionally. Gradually, a sea of change filled with turbulence enveloped her body. Clouds hovered over her life and over her entire body. Her life began growing darker and darker by the minute. Chances were, she could not understand that phase of her life. It made her very frightened. It was a feeling she was not equipped for neither educated enough for. Later on she read, this change is called 'adolescence'.

BB entered into this time in her life blindly with mixed and unexplainable emotions. The memories, the thoughts, the relationships, the disappointments which formulated the fabric of her childhood still linger. Daily, she felt as if a needle was pulling the threads of her body tighter and tighter in her life. She watched it weaving the fibers in many different textures with myriads of thread going under, over, up down, clockwise, counter clockwise and even spirally. In not so many words, growing up was really tough.

Being the second child of ten, BB had to assist in every area of the home with chores and provisions for food. These included tasks such as chopping big logs of wood from acacia prickly trees to be burned into coals in order to cook food and to sell. At that time, coal stoves were the only appliance used for cooking. Next, she had to lug big rocks to crack into fine stones to sell for the construction of concrete homes. The only means of transportation then was one's head or a donkey cart used by those who could have afforded one.

Other means of earning a living was fishing, diving conchs (of course, BB could not dive), rearing cows, pigs, chickens and digging crabs as a means of survival. Even though this kept her busy, she always found time a night a week to join her other brothers and sisters in fellowship, reading God's Word, making melody in songs and giving God praise and thanks for all He was doing for them in spite of the hardships she was facing. In the midst of it all, they loved each other and made themselves happy in their own way.

BB can never recall a day when her and her siblings ever fuss and fight amongst themselves. They laughed together and shared one another's joys and pain. They even cried together whenever one of them was being punished for something they did or did not do. This type of knitted relationship lasted for a while. Things continue to change due to lack of jobs in the country. This led to the migration of some of her family members to the neighboring islands to seek employment thus ending the brief moments of family togetherness. It was no more but every day she still thanks

God for those precious moments He had loan them – moments she will forever cherished.

After this brief side of BB's life had ended, independence crept in. Her life became very dull. She felt alone and confused. She did not have any secondary education so she took on added responsibilities, doing menial tasks for the elite in the society such as: cleaning and ironing, washing, styling and braiding hair, crocheting and doing embroidery to help herself financially as a teen.

As time went by, being the ambitious person, BB felt that this was not what she wanted to do for the rest of her life. She deserved better. The thought came, to take up private lessons to further educate herself and vowed that she would become a 'Nun' but boy oh boy what was she thinking. 'A Nun?' It sounded really good but her body was saying something else.

Another strange and new thing was maturing in her body. It was different. What was it? It had something to do with attraction of the opposite sex. Was she supposed to feel that way? Was it love or infatuation? She began questioning and doubting herself. What was it? Whatever it was, it felt good, strange but good. Whatever it was, BB was afraid to share or trust it with anyone and at the same time hoping that it will pass with time. Instead of the feeling going away, it became stronger and stronger. She tried on numerous occasions to distract herself by fantasizing on becoming a 'Star' rather than a 'Nun'. She spent countless hours secretly acting out Bible stories and reciting well – known poems. This however, began to expand. Her wish at that time came true. She began acting in church programs and entertainments, reciting on stage before an audience and singing in a little Church choir where she became a member in her town called "Quaint Paradise".

However, this lasted for a while, then "Thump!", BB's dream of becoming a star fell through whilst the strong attraction stayed. She became very shy, embarrassed and most of all afraid of young men. She desperately needed someone to talk to. Who was that someone? Where was that someone? She felt like a plot of dirt, like a neglected statue with overgrown weeds choking out the growth of what was good, useful and beautiful. Where was everyone?

Somewhere between the oldest child to the last of the ten, her parents love somehow seemed to have disintegrated because of stress and strain. She didn't know because of lack of communication in the family. Everything appeared like total chaos. All it took to make a happy family was love and communication. To be there, to hear about her successes, failures, moments of indecisions, feelings, reactions, opinions and responses during that crucial phase of the 'see – saw' moments of her life as a teenager which was termed as, 'Blind Contraventions'.

At the age of seventeen was the most difficult time of BB's life. It was then, she met and fell hopelessly in love with the most handsome youngster in her home town. For the first time in her life she began to experienced what she thought was real love. He was very short in stature and always wore a cute smile at least she thought it was. He too was very ambitious. Together they performed in many plays and entertainments. She felt as if she was in seventh heaven. At that age she was not allowed to date so she began sneaking around to see her Boaz but not what she wanted to do at all. Of course that spelt trouble.

BB's life continues to took a downward path. Scriptures reminded her that there is nothing hidden that will not be disclosed, and nothing hidden that will not be revealed or brought out into the open. This brought her back to reality. Knowing the town in which she lived and the community she envisioned trouble lurking around the corner waiting for her. The gossipers constantly fed false information to her parent causing both physical and emotional harm for her. It was she remembered these words, although the tongue weigh very little few people are able to hold it. This made her heedful of adults.

Negative thoughts skyrocketed. All BB wanted to do was run and keep on running away from it all. She blamed everyone that was in her path for was happening in her life even though she knew deep within it was really all her fault but did not know the danger of it. There she was in a situation, not educated for puberty, nor was she prepared for the changes in her body. Her pre-teen years, went by with no one to walk her through them. She did not possess the ability to cope with the new feelings. The ups, the downs, the round and round cycle she was experiencing. There was no caregiver to make sure that she was the well-rounded teen that she should be. She was lacking this kind of support that would not only allow her to explore, but also build her self-esteem and confidence for her future endeavors.

Day by day, BB would sit by a door or window and watch the morning glory opening their flowers and lifting their faces toward the sun. Day by day, she would sit with an aching heart green with envy watching other teenagers having fun, going places and doing things together with their parents wishing it was her. Why must they have all the fun? All she was yearning for was some quality time with someone like a mother, a teacher or an aunt perhaps, to help her understand life as a teenager indoors as well as outdoors. It was the togetherness, that quality time that counted. Instead all was shown was no empathy, neither did anyone acknowledge her distress, her groans, her pain or her intricacy.

There were times BB tried to initiate a conversation with a relative about the facts of life and about being a teenager but got a harsh response, smeared lips with hateful eyes peering at her. She was a victim by acts of deceit and manipulation both by peers and relatives. To sum it all up, she became a victim of "Blind Contravention".

Implanted on BB's heart were the words written, BB do not nurse hatred in your heart for anyone. Confront your neighbors directly so you will not be held guilty for their behavior. Never seek revenge or bear a grudge against anyone, but love your neighbor as yourself. All she needed to do was be of one mind, full of sympathy toward each other, loving one another with a tender heart and a humble mind but it was not so in BB's life.

After BB's dream of becoming a star shattered and her first love life crumbled, she felt uprooted and detached having no sense of direction. One bleak night, as she lay helplessly in bed searching for answers, searching for sleep and how she attends church regularly hoping that she would find answers to all of her questions, she still found none. Defiantly, she swore that once she was old enough to leave, she will never have to endure that kind of treatment and torment. Her life just kept on going blindly down one disastrous road after the other. The word 'Nun' resurfaced. Only this time, it stuck in her head like glue. The thought came, 'Why not go for it you are old enough to make your own decisions'. It was during that moment while her mind was chartering the flight through space in the dark of the night, her decision became final. She took that leap of faith.

Shortly after, at the age of eighteen, BB migrated to one of the neighboring islands. She had, had enough. Upon arrival, she immediately took up private lessons. She began studying very hard burning the midnight oil to meet her goal. For the second time in her life she failed. Her future began to revealed that, that was the biggest mistake ever made. She was forewarned that when things go wrong, don't go wrong with them but the advice went unnoticed. Something unexpected and detrimental took place in her life. Something that scarred her life forever. The answers you are looking for will be found in the next chapter.

To sum it all up, regardless of the circumstances, BB still thank God for making her, her. All she wanted was to be a bright and shining star with only one spark of illumination to resolve her life's problems. All she needed was just a candle to help her navigate that dark room in her afflicted heart to shine just like Jesus. He told BB that no matter what, let her light shine before men that they may see her good works and glorify her Father which is in heaven. Her flame extinguished because of:

1) "Blind Contravention" (as aforementioned)
2) She had not yet accepted the Lord Jesus Christ as her personal Lord and Savior – the True Light of the world. She knew of him but not really about him.

CHAPTER 3

DESERTED AND ALONE

My God, my God! Why have you forsaken me? Why do you remain so distant? Why do you ignore my cries for help? Every day I call to you, my God, but you do not answer me. Every night you hear my voice, but I find no relief. But I am a worm and not a man. I am scorned and despised by all! All they that see me laugh me to scorn: they shoot out the lip. (Psalm 22: 1-2; 6-7 (NIV)

As time rolled on, BB's health began to deteriorate. She began to feel weaker and weaker by the minute. Her eating habits decreased. Morning after morning she woke up with a bad feeling in her stomach. Her nights turned into days for lack of sleep. She could not understand what was happening in her body. As the sickness lingered and her body got weaker, she decided to visit a doctor.

After taking numerous tests he whispered, guest what BB you are pregnant dear. In shock she blurted out what is that? Looking surprised, he said in a concerned voice, "You are going to have a baby" she often heard the older folks say, this one or that one is having a baby but they never used the word pregnant so do forgive BB if she sounded green.

Mr. Fear then crept in. With her head hung down in shame and disgrace BB wept bitterly stuttering, "No! No! What have I done and how could this have happened? There she was in her early twenties and pregnant through ignorance and lack of knowledge. Most importantly, BB was forced upon by the baby's father in other words, she was 'Raped' only at that time she did not know what raped really was. She felt betrayed, ashamed and taken advantage of. She was faced with a situation in which she did not know what to do. She was trapped between a rock and a hard place.

Slowly, feeling dishonored, disrespected, discredit, stained, tainted and tarnished, BB got up out of the doctor's chair and walked dim-wittedly outside in the fresh air. She stood there speechless for a while not knowing in which direction to turn. Again she recognized that was the biggest of all the mistakes she has ever made. When she made that move, she thought it was for the better but things got worse. In a split second questions without answers flooded BB's mind as to what was she's going to tell her parents especially her mother. Did she make the words that were said to her come true that she will never be a lady? Where she was to go and to whom? Who was going to help her in the state that she was in?

BB wandered over a distance. After feeling exhausted, she stood under a shaded tree nearby a crooked path meditating. There she was all alone in a pool of water that came not from raindrops but from teardrops. Who could she have gone to and state her case that she was really dragged like a helpless animal and forced upon. "Who?" she said chokingly, who would believe her. She was even too embarrassed to tell anyone. Still not a Christian, she found herself all alone. The thought came to her in a sarcastic manner, BB you made your bed so lie in it.

Just imagine the dilemma in BB's life, when it became known publicly she was pregnant. Life at the homestead became unbearable. The situation forced her to leave and return to her hometown. She was greeted with prying eyes all around her. She almost could hear what the eyes were saying and their heart agreeing. This made her all the more uncomfortable, very uncomfortable. Like wild bush fire the bad news spread. She felt the heat of the flames burning her skin from a distance. She felt her heart racing through her body and pounding in her ears. Nervously, she staggered in the house, it was extremely cold, icy cold even though it was summer. She felt as if she was at the North Pole with its temperature below zero. She froze. That was, how unfriendly the atmosphere was. She was totally ignored. It was not a pretty sight. As the saying goes BB was left to paddle my own canoe.

It hurts to the point of numbness. No one seemed to care nor understood. She needed mercy and forgiveness from her loved ones. She wanted that bond they once shared. She was still the same. She made a mistake but, they were forbidden to converse with her. To her family, she had a bad dose of a contagious disease called "Disgrace" so they were afraid that they would have gotten contaminated so, they were isolated from her. She knew it was not easy for them by the expression on their faces. They were feeling her pain but their hands were tied so tight behind their back, holding them captive from touching or communicating with her.

No one ever came to questioned her situation not even up to this present time. She felt tired, fed-up, mixed up in mind and body. She felt stripped of her dignity. She felt like a homeless and an abandon child. She felt like a wounded soldier. She was at her lowest ebb. There she was barefooted and pregnant not knowing anything about it or what to do and what not to do. She felt totally like an outcast.

On numerous occasions she went to God in the stillness of the night thinking that because of her religious belief in Him, He would help her through this dilemma. She went on thinking that He had a place for her or a rock that she could crawl under and be at peace. In her thinking, she remembered all too well that her Heavenly Father do have a place for her where there are countless of warm blanketed arms filled with comforters of love. Love in which she could wrap herself in, feel relaxed, safe and not frightened. A place that is cozy and not bleak and lonely. At that time, BB thought being religious meant only praying and worshipping God but later learned that it was not so. All she was asking for was, when night came to be wrapped up and tangled up in God's blanket of love and protection which is Jesus Christ and feel his tender loving arms around her and sleep peaceably.

Way into the seventh month of BB pregnancy, an incident took place which she does not want or care to mention that nearly drove her to commit suicide. A wave of severe depression engulfed her from hunger, pain mixed with guilt, anger, loneliness, rejection, deep sadness, helplessness, hopelessness and regret too much to bear. The pain often became too much for her depressed state to bear. More than anything, all she wanted was the pain to end - to find closure, to be able to see the light at the end of a very lonely dark and mucky tunnel. She began listening to wrong voices. To her it seemed like the only choice. Deep inside, she knew it was not the answer but at that moment she felt like she could not move on with that kind of life anymore.

Suddenly, BB felt like blood was rushing to her head. She had to get away. Immediately, she got up and head for the nearby hills leading to the seaside to a more pleasant and peaceful atmosphere hoping and wishing her help would come from there. There, the trees became her refuge of escape. They became her altar and her cross. The sea became her tears. She stood by the water's edge away from everyone and everything. With her hands upon her head she screamed and screamed until there was no more voice left. A strong urge came over her to drown herself. To her, it was better if she died than lived. Instead, she just stood there while the waves taunted and teased her. She prayed aloud as she watched her tears bubbling gently on the water. She began to see that vast expanse of water as being her tears instead of an ocean. She felt like even God had forgotten and forsaken her. He was letting her down. She became a complete failure yet another time.

Feeling sore, starved and faint, BB began dragging through the thick bushes pushing, shoving at anything and everything that was in her way. The branches began lashing back at her for punishing them. She felt all battered, tattered and bruised. Without knowing or realizing how far she had walked, she sat down under a shaded sea grape tree. This gave her the opportunity to think where do she go from here. Her loved ones and friends stayed away from her. Her family stood at a distance.

In frustration BB cried out "Lord You must have an answer for me for I acknowledged my transgressions and my sin is always before me. Do not forsake me. Make haste help me. Listen to my cries for help. Night and day, I cry unto You. The tears fall hot upon my face and I know You see them. Please do not ignore them. For my heart is broken. I feel shattered and lost. I am only a traveler passing through. Spare me so I can smile again". Feeling exhausted and completely crushed with her heart beating wildly and her strength failing, BB fell into a sea of total darkness that was unlit not even by a ray of light, not even by a star.

Suddenly, BB was awakened by the sound of thunderous footsteps which made her frightened and fearful. It was a huge black cow. If that animal hadn't awakened her, she did not know what would have happened. Thank God for creating them. In an instant, she crawled and hid behind the tree until the animal disappeared then hastily began her long and tiresome journey home. It was almost dark so she was very frightened and afraid. On reaching home, without uttering a word, she disappeared into her little cell. She spent the night just lying there pondering over the day's events and wondering how long will she remain in this state of 'Desertion and Alone'. Sleep never came that night nor did she eat.

The time came for BB to go back to the neighboring island to give birth. On April, the twenty-second day of the year nineteen hundred and sixty- nine (1969) in the afternoon, she was transported to the hospital. There she was writhing to and fro in pain hoping that the nurse or doctor would make haste come to operate on her so that the pain would go away. That was what she thought was going to happen. She never knew how babies were born due to a lack of knowledge. Later on, she was told by a nurse that babies were not born that way unless there are complications. Again ignorance crept in.

BB were told by her parents used that babies came on airplanes or a big bird would drop them as mail when the time came for them to be born. At first she believed that story was true but as she grew older she knew that was not so. But still, did not know how they were born. Finding out that day made her feel nasty, dirty, cheap and also embarrassed. Her family never talked to her about the facts of life. So she found out in the most humiliating and degrading way. To them, talking about that topic was indecent, obscene, filthy and vulgar. That night was a complete shock to her. Later on that night she gave birth to twins a boy and a girl.

She never knew she was having twins. Things were so tough for her that she only had one pack of diapers, one pack of two baby pins and one pack of t-shirts for two children.

Upon BB's discharged, the time came for her to go back to her home town, this time not alone. Not with one baby but two. Just when she thought things could not get any worse, worse came. She had no help. She had no one. There were days she had to go back to burning coal and beating fine rocks to sell to support her children and herself. She was abandoned completely. Sometimes the babies would cry at nights and not knowing what to do or what was happening to them she would sit with one on one shoulder and the other on the next and cried along with them. This kind of treatment continued until one day she was told she had to leave the house and find somewhere else to live. For peace, she agreed then left not knowing where they were going. They were homeless for a while. Later on in the day Mr. Goodness and Mr. Mercy followed her and she was taken in by one of her aunts who finally recognized and heard her plea for help.

During that time, she was not hearing from the babies' daddy Jas, he had left the island without even seeing them. After two years, he returned home, requesting to marry her and she agreed but his decision was blocked by his mother so, he became the 'Sugar daddy' in town forgetting all about his responsibilities. He was not really ready to be a father.

Money then became a big problem for BB. That was really scary. She was left to support her babies by herself. She spent countless days toiling to make ends meet. Many days she had to go without in order for them to survive. She tried her best not to fantasize too much about their father being a part of their lives. Her babies deserved better, way better than that. She came to the conclusion that, anyone who refrained from taking on his or her burden is good-for-nothing and wrong for her. She was learning this the hard way. So, she worked from sun to sun and that was her solitude. She believed that the Lord was testing her. She believed then that the Lord was not going to put more on her than she can bear.

Finally, BB felt like a yoyo or a puppet on a string. She felt like the game entitled 'Spin the top', just going round and round; up and down; to and fro; back and forth' swaying here and swaying there. She was still asking God for his help but still refusing to let Him be a part of her life. Here, she wanted her cake and eat it at the same time. All that was left to say, she was seduced by the false gods of insecurity, unpredictability, isolation, desertion abandonment, alone and exclusivity.

What more surprises her life had in store for her. You will soon find out just keep on reading.

CHAPTER 4

ALL THAT GLITTERS IS NOT GOLD

Husbands love your wives just as Christ loved the Church and gave himself up for her to make her holy, cleansing her by the washing with water through the Word. To present her to himself as a radiant church, without stain or wrinkle or any blemish, but holy and blameless. In this same way, husbands ought to love their wives own body.

He who loves his wife loves himself. (Ephesians 5:25–28) (LASB)

However, this did not ring true for BB. Why? The answers you will find written within the following pages.

After two and a half years of struggles with her twin babies, their father Jas once again agreed to marry her. She quickly accepted his proposal again. It was for real this time. To her then, it was the only way out of her imprisonment, slavery, emotional abuse and suffering so she thought. In ancient times, when a young lady birthed babies out of wedlock, parents, relatives and older persons in the community looked upon her as an outcast, a nobody, a reject, poison, a disgrace or a stumbling block. So, despite his unfair treatment, BB happily accepted.

The long awaited day finally arrived. It was the seventeenth day of July, nineteen hundred and seventy – one. It was the happiest day of her life. It was 'The Day' when wedding bells were going to chime, rejoicing with her. Butterflies were dancing all inside and around her. Still in the midst of their sweet buzzing sound, was a still small voice at the back of her head saying, 'Why are you so anxious to marry a man who refused to take care of his responsibilities?' The thought wrestled with her for a while. Then out loud she echoed, 'Why not? I am looking for a safe haven.' Apart from that, it is for my honor and my respect in the eyes of my parents and the community. She thought it was the right thing to do at that time.

She was sick and tired of living a tedious life. She was still young. Suddenly, her thoughts were interrupted by a parade of honking horns from an early morning wedding. Unable to go back to sleep, she got up and began to pace the floor backward and forward with a nervous tingling sensation enveloping her body. She began to busy herself doing what she did not know.

Time began to move like lightning. Without realizing it, the time had arrived. BB got dressed in the most beautiful milky – white flowing gown she had ever seen with her forehead filled with dancing jet-black curls. She felt like an angel just waiting for its wings, its Halo. A horn blew. She trembled. It was her driver. She was then being escorted to the church in a black ford vehicle. She arrived a little earlier than scheduled. She sat quietly in the parked car for a while just gazing hopelessly at the crowd marching in droves in the church. It was time. Time for her to march up the aisle.

Slowly, BB slid out of the car and walked nervously to the door of the church. Shockingly, she stood still with her mouth gaped open. What a lovely sight it was to behold! Her heart skipped a beat. Inside the sanctuary, starting from the walls, to the pews, to the altar were exquisitely decked in pink and white roses, bells, ribbons and bows with shades of black here and there. It was elegantly done in co-ordination with the gowns of the bridesmaids and the tailor - made tuxedos of the groom and groomsmen.

The edifice was packed to capacity with human figures looking all posh. Outstanding among them were her superiors from her work place – the Navy Officials neatly uniformed in their chalky – white naval suits thus adding the icing to the cake. The reverberating sound of 'Here comes the Bride' intercepted her moment of mesmerism. It was a feeling of tranquility.

Into this serene panorama, BB gracefully sauntered down the aisle with bouncing lifting strides on her father's arm to the bridal march as it serenaded her on the low silk rolling carpet blanketed snugly between the crowded pews with little pink and white petals sprinkled all over. As she walked, she felt all eyes on her. The church became her haven but as she strutted down the aisle, she heard faint groans and moans she did not understand. Were they sending her a message? Whatever it was, it sent chills up her spine but refused to let it spoil her moment of bliss. Yet, at the same time she was still trying to understand the challenges she was now confronted with.

On reaching the altar, BB felt like a polished swan nestled in the midst of a flock of pink flamingoes on one side and a nest of well-groomed robust eagles on the other. The crowning beauty of this tableau was the repeating of vows and exchanging of rings. This outward demonstration of commitment made at the altar before

God and humanity that day, were not entered into lightly by her but with an honest desire, to do everything humanly possible to make her marriage work and destined it to stay that way with the promise made; 'Until death do us part'. Her vows became the cornerstone of her marriage. On that day she never knew such happiness existed. It was a moment in her life she would never forget.

Wow! Three months into the marriage BB became a teacher and pregnant again thus, ending her heavenly Elysium. Just when she was on the verge of a new start in her life, her dream life shattered all over again. Suddenly, from a distance the whistling sound of a volcano in all its fury erupted. Storms clouds rolled in, tempers flared, feelings were hurt, misunderstandings arouse and all communications ceased. This was her marriage described in one paragraph. The proverbial safety net began to drop life-sized holes from the lava and brought along intense heat.

Daily, shocking experiences began to unmask. Jas justified his temper. His mood altered. He became involved with extra-marital affairs. Within minutes BB began to see a complete different side of the man she married she never knew existed. Was she that blind? Or was it that she refused to see the red flag waving 'Danger Ahead' in the midst of the darkened sky? She thought she had hit the 'Jackpot filled of glittering gold, where did it go? She later learnt that it was not real gold not even gold-plated but pure fake.

BB quickly remembered the groans and moans made in the Chapel as she walked up the aisle. They were then unspoken messages of caution. She soon discovered that he was not the man he pretended to be but just a human in disguise. Things just kept on getting worse. She also discovered that he had another serious problem which resulted in lies and more lies, violence, anger, bitterness, swearing, yelling sarcastic insults at her. There were times he would come home and act in an irrational manner throwing objects all over the place. Oftentimes his words were very harsh and very hurtful and he did not care. Hurting her became his specialty. Due to his erratic behavior, BB was unable to defend herself, to find relief or unable to rise above it or compete with the unexpected nightmare encounters, which replaced her. Whenever she questioned him, he would, as the expression goes, 'Fly off the handle' and lose control. So, she resolved to keep quiet and take it all. She had learned when to speak and when to be silent.

About five months, into her pregnancy, BB began experiencing physical symptoms like severe headaches and ulcers, symptoms of anxiety, panic attacks, depression and eating disorders. Oftentimes suicidal thoughts again resurfaced and intrusive thoughts and images of the past haunted her. She became devastated by such experience.

The answer is, BB had entered into this relationship being inexperienced. Because of this, she did not know what signs to look for that would indicate something was wrong or will be. The man she married took advantage of her vulnerability. However, she did not let the problems she was experiencing hinder her from doing her job the best she knew how.

In the midst of all that chaos, God had allowed her to give birth to a healthy baby boy. Two months after his birth, she was severely beaten and had to flee for her life with her baby bundled in her arms. Her spouse caught up with her, putting a knife to her throat and ordered her back to the house and then left. Upon reaching the house BB laid the innocent little bundle on the bed, dropped to her knees with her head in her hands and wept uncontrollably.

A year later, she was chosen to go to abroad to college to further her studies to upgrade her teaching career. This made her very happy to get away but it didn't work because the harassing phone calls kept on coming. But thank God He was there with her because in spite of the torment she passed with distinction. She paused here to say, "What God has for you it is for you" and no man or no one can take it away.

At that time, they were living with a family of ten all adults. They all knew what was going on and pretended to care when they did not. Their faces, their attitudes, indicated otherwise. In their adversities they rejoiced among themselves in little gatherings. They talked about her in earshot range. They attacked and tore at her secretly. They blamed her for things she knew not of. Tales that were not true were told to her spouse which contributed to her bad treatment. They encouraged him with adultery and fornication in front of her eyes. Sometimes she wondered how could people be so cruel to one another. This was all new to her.

BB felt like an Israelite living in an Egyptian territory. She felt as if she was living in the midst of centipedes, scorpions and vipers. She would even dream about the crawly creatures, night after night until she felt like they were actually crawling all over her, grabbing, nipping and stinging her flesh. 'Ouch!' Even though God had given her the power to walk on snakes and scorpions, power that is greater than the enemy has, so nothing can harm or hurt her, she did not possess it because of her weakness and wavering relationship with him.

There were times she was afraid to go out for fear of what people would be thinking about her. She did not have the wisdom and the knowledge at that time to understand at that time that we must be more concerned with what God thinks rather than about what people thinks. This where BB failed. Again she was faced with the reminder that although the tongue weighs very little, few people are able to hold it. She needed the Lord to send her a miracle because He was the only one who always hears. She desperately needed a friend with a listening ear.

The Word of God instills in us that Jesus is our only friend, a friend who walks in when the world walks out. He is a friend who sticks closer than a brother. Solomon in Proverbs reveals that when things go wrong don't go wrong with them. BB was for peace but when she spoke, everyone around her was for war.

In nineteen seventy-seven opportunity presented itself again for BB. She was given another chance to attend a University in England. In that year she felt at peace. No one was bruising her body. As for the phone calls it was difficult getting through back then and letters took forever to reach. BB was able to work with ease and again performed well with a star beside her name indicating that she was selected to further her studies in completing her degree course in education. However, this never came into being due to lack of government funds so she was told. The time came for her to go back to her agonizing life. She was never again given the opportunity to do her degree course.

On returning home, life seemed to hold and offer so very little for BB daily. Everything angered her. Nothing seemed to satisfy her. Nothing gave her pleasure. Everything was boring and irritating. She desperately needed to get away again. After looking in the mirror and seeing a frame with a deep hollow in its shoulders, eyes sunken into its head steering sadly at her, made her frightened. In desperation, she suggested to her spouse that it was time to move from where they were living and live on their own as a real family. He needed to shoulder his own responsibility. He was living too good with his wife and children out of the picture. Surprisingly, he agreed. Within weeks they relocated but in the same neighborhood.

In the year nineteen eighty-seven, BB was severely beaten with a chair. This resulted with a broken wrist, bruised feet and numerous cuts and bruises. In addition, every appliance she owned was hammered and destroyed. Her entire wardrobe and personal belongings were set on fire. There she was walking on her toes of one bandaged foot and down on the heels of the other bandaged foot while her left arm was in a heavy cast. What an awful picture. She decided she had had enough and left him. Soon, they found ourselves together again but in a different neighborhood.

For a long time, BB had kept this part of her life a secret from her family. When asked about her accident she said a big black cat made her fall. Why didn't she expose Jas for who he really was? Why did she lie? Those were questions she is still baffling with. Being a school teacher, this handicap hindered her from attending the graduation exercises at the school where she taught.

After experiencing much pain, BB had to visited a doctor again and decided to tell him the truth but he had already figured it out from his findings. This reminded her that the truth to a lie always reveals itself in some way or the other. So, it is always good to speak the truth no matter what it cost. The doctor then made a decision to send her to another country to seek further treatment. Whilst there, in the dark of the night as she lay gazing up at the black empty space, thinking about her life, she reached out to God. She began to cry out with all her heart, her soul and her strength the old hymn "Father I stretch my hands to Thee no other help I know. If Thou withdraws thyself from me oh, whither shall I go?

BB's outlook on life needed to change and only God was the one to do so. She decided to pray asking the Lord to enter into her heart and take full possession of her life that by His grace she will overcome her depressed moods. She continued to asked for His full measure of contentment and patience and create in her a clean heart and renew a right spirit within her. Create in her a greater willingness to forget self and stand on, the many promises of His Word which is the key to her open door to a more satisfying and happier life and marriage. She further asked Him to release her from her frustrations and if He is testing her give her the strength to endure the test. Help her to know that godliness with contentment comes from Him and Him alone. That night, BB confessed her sins and believed in her heart that Christ died for her sins and asked for God's forgiveness. She invited Him into her heart and made Him her Lord and Savior. BB Thank God for the Cross. Amen! That was the night BB gave her life to the Lord and whatever happened from then on would be completely out of her hands and now placed into God's hand.

That night BB also sought intimacy with God. She confessed her complacency and apathy and received Jesus Christ into her life as her personal Lord and Savior. BB then felt different and refreshed. She knew she had made the right choice. It gave her the satisfaction that was the only way out and only God, through his son, Jesus Christ could fill the emptiness she felt inside and only Him could save her from that tortured life. That night, God became her refuge her pillar of strength. She fell sound asleep. BB awakened the next morning with a new attitude toward life. She made a promised never to let the world make her a nobody. For, in God's Kingdom there are no nobodies we are all a somebody. This time, she returned home a completely different person. This time she was not alone. God was with her.

BB finally reached my destination. Whilst driving home, she was attacked by her estranged spouse. Just when he was about to hit her, his hand paused in midair. Right there and then, she knew that God's presence was still with her. At that moment she smiled. All she needed was the strength to conquer Satan completely. Later that night after calming down, she related her revelation to him hoping that it will change him. They talked way into the wee hours of the morning about the abusive relationship. He made promises after promises that he would change. They decided to seek counseling from a local Pastor. That they did. He acknowledged and admitted for the first time that he had a problem and had a violent temper and begged for help.

The sessions did not last long. Jas reverted to his old ways. BB was accused of having an affair with the same Pastor who was counselled them. She felt very embarrassed. BB was victimized in the name of the Lord but it gave her the fortitude to keep on praying. She refused to let the devil win again. Prayers were her meat night and day. It was the only thing that kept her going. Years rolled on and the conditions remained the same.

Many times, when the children went to sleep, in the wee hours of the night, BB would walk the streets crying, praying and quoting appropriate scriptures from God's Word. Sometimes, she would sit on one of the neighbor's porch until the breaking of day. She lived near a Baptist church and sometimes she would go there very late at night all alone after being beaten and crying out in pain and anguish to God. She felt as if her faith was failing her.

She was getting weak. For the second time leaving Jas entered her mind. Then she began to see a different picture. If she keeps on leaving him that means she was failing as a wife and as a mother. So she stayed.

There were times BB was afraid to say anything to him because he was like an elevator button. Sometimes he will be up and in good spirits and sometimes down in the dumps. The time came for her to say goodbye to a failed marriage. After running up and down, BB left him again and stayed with a relative. She made up her mind to tell her family the truth about her constant abuse. At that time her children were well advanced in years. The eldest had already left home to seek a livelihood elsewhere. This left her last son in the crossfire. (Will elaborate more on children in one of my other chapters).

Moving away from her relative BB fled somewhere far away where he could not find her. Living there was not easy. She was very unhappy and uncomfortable. Her mind was always on her son she left behind because he was still in High School and it was nearing his graduation. There was no one there to help him in his studies so after a year, she returned home.

Jas and BB got back together. (Lord help her). They had a fresh start. Everything was going well. Again they talked about their problems and again he admitted that he had changed and this time their marriage is going to work. Did she believe him? Not really, but she gave him the benefit of the doubt. Some mornings he would get up very early and clean both outside and inside the house and even sometimes cook. They began doing things together without fighting all the time. They started going places together like fishing, walking on the beach, socializing with friends mostly his, because he didn't allow her to have friends nor would he allow her to associate with any members of her family. It was not because he said so, but for peace and contentment. She felt great. She decided to stop complaining about everything and tried to be a friend and a supporter to him. She realized she was fighting a demonic spirit.

BB began to think how can she bring God into his life? She started by using that opportunity to try the traditional approaches. BB began reading her Bible in front of him. Then she took it a little further and read with him and also prayed with him. Everything was going smoothly. BB re-applied for a teaching post and was accepted. She felt on top of the world then 'Boom! the world was on top of her.

One day Jas came home the worse she had ever seen him. She became very fearful. In the twinkling of an eye it seemed as if a bomb had exploded scattering its shells all over her. She plunged from an emotional high to an emotional low. Then it hit her he never changed at all, it was all a farce. She knew then that he could not overcome that habit on his own. She went to his family for help but they refused by saying he doesn't need any help and she thinks he is crazy. She was in that alone. She felt like she was thrown into a field and told to harvest without any tools or a sickle. It was like being hungry and unable to eat.

BB's life was going on a downward spiral. Its sudden shift threw her off balance. Her life was turned upside down but Jesus promise that he would never leave her nor forsake her especially when situations in her life shifted. Within that time frame, her last son got graduated and was hired as a Custom Officer and then transferred to one of the neighboring islands leaving BB all alone with a raging demented man.

After her son on left, things worsened so much that she was afraid to close her eyes at night. Again she began to doubt God. There were nights Jas would come home and just stand over her steering with fierce eyes, breathing hard and fuming at the mouth. All BB could have done was just lie still without moving. God help her if she should as much move a finger or even wriggled a toe, he would pick her up like a kite and throw her like a ping-pong ball and wherever she landed she landed. If she happened to cry out in pain, he would kick her into oblivion. This had happened many times. Too numerous to count.

At times, gigantic fears would loom over her. BB discovered that the longer she cringed and shied away from it, the bigger the giants became. The problem was, just too big and too hot to handled. She found herself in it over my head. It was too frightening. She left her plight in the Lord's hands resting beneath His sheltering arms. She felt like a tiny straw, no matter which way she turned there was no way of escape. The walls of tragedy were closing in. The weight was so unbearable. BB was breaking under the load. She learned that she was not going to solve any of her problems until she let go and let God.

Very early one morning after being beaten, BB quietly slipped out of bed sore and blackened, limped toward an elevated rocky hill leading to the beach with the intent to kill herself again. As she tottered along she felt like a way-faring traveler carrying a loaded bag filled with problems much too heavy to drag or lift. Its contents were, fear, loneliness, rejections, anger, hate, prejudice, inferiority, depression, heartache, hurt, pain, moodiness and bitterness. At the same time Jesus was saying to her, to cast all her cares upon him for He cares for her. He was encouraging her to be still and know that He is God. He was encouraging BB his weary traveler as she dragged on, to lay aside every heavy weight that so easily beset her so she could run the race of freedom, the race of peace and assured her of his love. He was telling her not to fear for as a father pity his children so will He pity her.

Slowly as BB reached the rocky hill, she gently made her way over the jagged precipice while the wind heedlessly tore at her skin through to her heart. Carefully, she lowered her painful body under its shelter. As she sat there just listening to the sound of the wind and the beating of the waves, her heart began to hum the old hymns 'Rock of ages clef for her, let me hide myself in Thee ". Then she remembered another one of her favorites in the dark of the midnight while the storms howl above her and there's no hiding place just keep her safe until the storms passes by.

Even though BB tears fell like torrents of rain at that moment she felt safe in the hollow of that unyielding rock where no earthly storms could enter and wishing that she could stay there until the storms of her life subsided. Also, where the sun will shine turning her landscape into a place of peaceful calm. For the second time BB felt at rest and at peace. God had provided his everlasting arms in the clef of that rock to cover her. Dazed from her sheltered experience, she heard the voice of Jesus say, come unto me and rest Lay down thy weary head lay down upon my breast and rest. Gradually BB lifted herself up out of the valley and wobbled on to the beach humming as she goes Precious Lord take her hand lead her on let me stand, she is tired, she is weak and she is worn.

As she walked, she remembered these words an elderly lady once told her whenever she goes to the beach, dig a hole and empty all her problems in it then cover it over and let it wash away into the sea of forgetfulness. Immediately she took her advice and began to dig. BB mentally dug a hole purposely throwing sand and dirt out until it was very deep. With eagerness, she emptied all the offences, problems, abuse, and sorrows that wounded her. Quickly with her hands, she shoveled the sand over it whispering a prayer as she labored then, briskly walked away.

When she got home Jas was still asleep. She crept quietly into bed and fell into a deep peaceful sleep. When she awakened he was gone, where? she did not know nor did she really care. BB began to pray aloud for him because at that moment she believed that God could move in his heart wherever he was and no matter the situation, make him a new creature. She did not know what else to do or where else to go for help. No support systems were available. Jas had taken away her love, her self-esteem, her self-respect, her dignity, her individuality and her values. The law refused to help by saying that it was a domestic problem. So, BB placed her trust in God for she knew when no one else cares He cares.

The remainder of my days with Jas, BB suffered in silence. She went about as if she had a perfect marriage, laughing and singing praises unto God. Until one night she was called from the altar of a church while she was requesting prayers for him she refused to leave. When she got home Jas was waiting for her and he sure battered her with a pressing iron. This still did not stop her from praising and serving her God who brought her out of the miry clay and set her foot on a rock to stay. That was what kept her going day by day because whenever she was around Jas, she knew that she was sitting on a time bomb just waiting to explode.

One Friday, the thirteenth day of August, nineteen ninety-three, BB literally saw death flash before her eyes. Tradition calls it 'Black Friday' whenever the thirteenth of a month falls on a Friday. She thought her life was over. On that sad night, she heard heavy running footsteps. Peeping through the drapes of her home, she saw it was her husband running, panting and out of breath.

He jumped the barb wired fence and like the Incredible Hulk burst through the window and without saying a word pounced upon her like a beast on its prey. He kept on punching, kicking and biting her all over making sounds like a roaring lion. She tried to escape. She managed to reach outside the door catching up with her, he pushed her on to the concrete and began choking her.

There BB was struggling and gasping for breath. No one came. She began to see stars. She felt the breath leaving her body. She felt faint. Once again God gave her a little strength to free herself. Helplessly, she dragged herself to the closet fence calling for help. Still the loud fearful screams brought no one to my rescue. Suddenly, she felt a blow to her head. It sent her reeling. Jas reached for her and dragged her toward the house. Fear crept over her. She was livid afraid to go inside for fear she might not come out alive.

Realizing she was fighting a losing battle, she gave up. There were no more tears, no more strength left. Feeling weak and faint, her body all battered, bruised and covered in blood, her night dress hanging in bloody rags, she collapsed to the ground with him still punching her. There and then, she hoped that God will take her home out of all this misery where there would be no more sorrow, no more pain. She had, had it. That was the last straw.

She did not know how long she was lying there when she felt hands, soft hands lifting her up. BB thought she was dreaming but it really was hands lifting her up like Angels hands. Then she heard a faint voice whispering in her ear saying, everything is going to be alright and was carried in the house and given a cup of hot tea. Drifting in and out of consciousness, she saw it was his mother with tears streaming down her cheeks. Later that night, she was taken to the hospital treated and then released early the next morning.

Upon her release, BB fled to another island nearby all blackened and blue, bruised ribs, bruises, cuts and teeth marks from bites all over her skin. She ran leaving everything behind. When the aircraft lifted off the airstrip, BB began to thank God over and over again and again. She vowed not to look back and that she did. After reaching her final destination, she had to visit a doctor again. She was unable to do anything but just lie there in pain and a broken heart. Then it came to her that God can also heal broken hearts but He wants all the pieces. From that day on God had all of her.

To the readers, after you read this chapter, if you do not have a relationship with God, now is the time to seek one. For it was only Him who had brought BB through that terrible ordeal. She guessed the question is being asked, why did she stay with Jas that long. A period of twenty-two years of unmitigated hell. Why didn't she leave him a long time ago? Folks it does not work that way. She can now boast that she left with the satisfaction of knowing that she had given it her all to make her marriage work. She tried many different strategies and failed. She believed in second chances. Think about the many chances God has and still is giving us. Many were surprised at Jas behavior because out in the community he was a 'Yes ma'am, Yes Sir, No ma'am, No sir' kind of guy. Now BB is here to tell you that 'All that glitters are not gold'.

CHAPTER 5

BRUISED REEDS AND SMOKING FLAX

In Isaiah 53:5 (KJV), God's Word declares: He was wounded for our transgressions. He was bruised for our iniquities; the chastisement of our peace was upon Him; and with His stripes we are healed.

In not so many words, God is saying that the iniquity of the fathers is passed down to the children. So, if we do not deal with the iniquity of our lives, we will see it repeated in the lives of our children. Satan wants us to keep in the dark so he can continue to have power and control over us and our children. God's Word tells us that Satan comes to kill, steal, and destroy. That was exactly what he was trying to do to BB's children.

BB, protecting her most precious Reeds was the most challenging responsibility she endured during her turmoil. She did not only have to protect them from the demonic forces that were invading her home but also from forces in the community.

Like David, BB mourn for her children. She felt isolated because of her childhood experiences. She lacked a positive mental picture of good parenting. She had limited understanding of parent-child relationships. Because of her abusive situation, she often became overwhelmed, frustrated and engaged in abusive discipline in her parenting. This treatment exhibited high levels of stress and discord in the lives of her children often as a result of the chaotic and unhealthy home environment in which they were a part.

They spent all of their youthful years watching from a distance as their father inflicted bodily harm on their mother. They spent numerous and numerous days listening to the crude insults and obscene language ringing in their ears. That became a part of their growing up. Therefore, they began to experience high levels of anxiety and became emotionally overloaded. They often felt responsible for the abuse and began to show intense feelings of helplessness.

Sometimes when they would see their mother just lying there writhing in pain, they would try to interfere to protect her, thus putting themselves at risk. There were times when they were afraid to help. So, they would just lay there and stifled moans and groans with silent tears slithering down their innocent faces as they listened to her screams and pleas for help, unable to move or do anything. At other times afraid to cry out loud for fear he would turn on them.

Oftentimes with tear-stained faces, BB would see them out of the corner of her eye helplessly staring at her. Their facial expressions explained it all. They were desperately watching for answers or for indications as what to do to prevent their father's outburst. The truth of the matter was, she had none to give. They were strangers in their own home. Soon he began to treat them like property to be used at his disposal. He would brutally punish them to get at her, making them more fearful of him. Whenever he began to shout at them they would tremble at the sound of his voice. It was as if a gush of howling wind had come across rocking the house to and fro tearing it up from its foundation. Here BB was crying out to God to show her His love and save her as He have promised. When BB suffered, His promises comforted her. They gave her life.

BB's children became like 'Bruised Reeds and Smoking Flax'. She called them her 'Reeds' because they were parts of her joints that connect the pipes and reeds to her heart and the 'Flax' that weaves the lining of her heart and lights it up. Consequently, these two, 'Bruised Reeds and Smoking Flax' combined, made up the state of her poor distressed children. They came to a stage where they were very bruised and broken. Their spark of hope was being threatened by doubts and fears rising from their nightmare experiences. They became sensible to sin and misery which made them as smoking flax. The flame from the smoking flax was partially lit within, smothering their life.

They were like starlings, frightened every time Jas appeared and even at every passerby. They were despised, rejected and treated like pieces of trash lying on the ground. As a result, they displayed intense emotions of tears, anger, bitterness, frustration and even cynicism. They became withdrawn, isolating themselves from everyone close to them. Sometimes, they had difficulty sleeping at nights. Their appetite changed. They appeared to have very low self-esteem. At that time, BB felt that the hurt, which was so indelibly printed on the minds of her 'Reeds' would never be erased. To her, they sometimes seemed weaker than bruised reeds and smoking flax.

This observation also made BB very weak. There were times she wanted to cry out aloud but stifled it instead she had to maintain a brave front. She had to be strong for her children. So often she was constrained to say, "I would, but cannot help, I would, but cannot pray, I would, but cannot love". What she really wanted to convey to them was that she could not do any of these because of her weakness. Her hands were tied too tight.

Deep sorrow entered her home and within her reeds. BB's impulse was to take them into a secluded room and sit down in despair amid the wrecks of their hopes and dreams and cry together. She did not know what the devil was trying to do to them. She really needed God during this fiasco of a life her and her children were living. There were days she needed a vision from God for her family and herself for they were tiring fast.

At that time, she was no use to her bruised reeds. She felt like a speck of dust in a sunbeam. She was like a dead plank in the home. The bruised reeds were like the pillars in the house where everyone leaned causing numerous of potholes making them all dirty and corroded from the ills of the home. She felt exhausted. The mental fatigue she was experiencing was almost more than she could bear. Whenever she closed her eyes, her thoughts plow into one another, her mind raced from one question to another. She really needed a good night's sleep. Every night, she felt as if she was fighting with her pillow. Then she would whisper, "Lord, what are the uses of my broken reeds when they are not suitable enough to bend and make sweet music and only could produce discordance?" They were all burnt out and scorched walking around daily with scared faces from the burning flax.

The pain BB felt, insinuated that the whip of injustice will never stop. It just kept on lash after lash. Although she howled out constantly 'Lord, stop the whip and give me a little respite', instead it came down, with its cruel thong, lash after lash. Whenever BB lay down, all she saw was ghosts in the room hovering over her. Ghosts of abuse, ghosts of shame and embarrassment. When she stared in the dark of the midnight, she saw the black form of death starring back at her, cynically saying, 'Thou art my prey. I shall have thee. I must have thee. The scene was like 'Hell on earth' or on wheels burning waiting to engulf her and her bruised reeds. She blurted out: "God, if this continues any longer, I will perish leaving my loved ones behind to suffer". She began to yell out in desperation, 'Oh! My 'Bruised Reeds Satan will not break you'. Please reeds, help me to help you by putting your trust in God. Let your conviction be strong enough to break thy hurt and ease your pain altogether so she would not die and leave them all behind. If you do this, God will surely bring you out of this fire unbroken and unharmed like the three Hebrew boys in the fiery furnace removing the aching void the world cannot fill, into a life of peace and joy.

Oh! How BB longed to see that day when God would plant her reeds by the rivers of living waters in fertile soil and watch them grow into sturdy, peaceful mahogany trees, whose leaves will never whither, watering them every moment of every day because they felt inadequate, out of place and unwanted. Now they have grown into their adolescence stage of torment and turmoil.

The worst mistake for her reeds was to be around a constant state of warfare. Absorbing it all, they grew up confused, hurt and angry. This affected their attitude. They began to act out this anger and confusion inappropriately, to their friends, teachers, other authorities and parents in an aggressive and cruel manner. BB began to see a pattern forming in their lives from the traits of their father. She began receiving numerous complaints about the sons especially the young one.

BB tried stealing some precious moments with her bruised reeds while Jas was out of the house. She did this by reading Bible stories, praying with them and playing some board games together to see if that would help the situation. She also used the opportunity to talk to them about the dangers of life the best she knew how and about the situation they were facing in the home. Because of this, they grew up with behavioral problems that were unacceptable in school as well as in society. It affected their ability to learn and hindered their progress to excel. Her youngest son always complained with serious headaches and was unable to study the way he should. These disabilities stemmed from the nomadic life we lived. Roaming from place to place going from one neighbor's house to the next for refuge and safety.

BB's children also manifested a myriad of disorders into adulthood. For example, post-traumatic stress, panic and anxiety, mood swings and substance abuse problems. She wanted many times to leave and get a divorce. It seemed as if it was the only solution that would ease the pain. She became guilty of the fact that it was all her fault. She did not move them away from that hostile environment in time. She grew with the mentality that marriage, no matter what state it is in, should last forever. She blamed herself for their mental state.

Another reason was her mother Sal, she always said to her, 'to be married is to have a good name and it is honorable in society' so, she tried to hold on to it but to her that statement was completely wrong. There she was, staying in a brutal marriage for the sake of her mother Sal and for the sake of the children. A marriage that was extremely detrimental and had no merit at all but agony, torment and a relationship where no love was ever displayed.

This was the second time love was absent in her life, now, it is being passed down to her children. BB did not know what love really was and how to love. The only thing she ever was taught about love was Jesus loves her because the Bible says so me and God so loved the world, that He gave His only begotten son, that whosoever believeth in him should not perish but have everlasting life taught to her in Sunday School. She taught them to her children the same way, but that was not enough. They needed the love of their parents as well. How was she able to show her children that kind of love and affection they so desperately longed for, when, all they did was run, run, run for their life. They were paying the price for her failed marriage and nothing she did could have restored and replaced the security of a stable home in their life.

In retrospect, BB's children also grew up in an unstable environment where empathy and trust were lacking, so, they sprouted up living a ravaged adulthood. They were crippled by mixed messages and family secrets. When asked about their childhood, they replied, we had none. It was like living in a 'Wrestler's domain'. BB began seeing the same pattern of anger emerging from them. Her daughter Beth, built a wall around herself shutting out everyone and no one could have penetrated. She slipped behind a mask of defiance and refused to acknowledge what was going on around her. She crept into a shell. Her father did not allow her to go anywhere, nor did he allow her to mix and mingle with friends and family.

There was an incident where he had beaten her so savagely with a block of wood leaving a nail in her left hand and had to be rushed to the hospital. This took place just before her graduation. Shortly after she graduated, she was taken abroad to a foreign country by her grandmother Belle, her father's mother, to live with one of her aunts. This too, did not go very well. She was treated the same way by them like an outcast not only physically but also emotionally. There were days when she was unable to eat due to the tension and constant accusations. The treatment became so strenuous and severe, that it drove her to attempt suicide and for the second time in her life had to be rushed to the hospital arriving just in time for the doctors to save her.

After her recovery, things grew from bad to worse. So, she fled to another part of the same country leaving everything behind. They refused to give her any of her belongings. She was stripped of everything she owned by them. She was bereft. After she left, life for her became much better until she married and gave birth to two beautiful babies a son and a daughter. About three months into marriage, things changed again. She spent many nights driving here and there out in the wilderness with her children, going nowhere and not fearing the dangers that were surrounding them. She sometimes slept in her car. There were times when she would just travel long distances and for long periods of time without anyone knowing of her whereabouts. After eight years of instability she left. This time she did not return. Up to this day, the cause of her leaving remains a mystery.

BB oldest son Zed, her twin, turned to substance abuse. He went from a size thirty-two in waist to a size eight. His features changed beyond recognition. Whenever she saw him it gave her a sharp pain in her chest. Not because of his condition but what drove him to the condition. He is very intelligent and is not afraid to try anything his hands finds to do and was very good at it. He was a regular church-goer and was very active. Because of this evil demon, he lost it all. BB tried on several occasions to talk to him but failed her mission.

Then, there was her last son Jabez (now deceased) became a child of rage. He married his high school sweetheart and they both produced three children. He grew to be very abusive not only in the home but out in the community as well. Like his father, his family was in constant turmoil and jeopardy fleeing for their life. During his outrageous outburst, he always used his mother as his reason for hurting his family for how his father treated her. This hurt BB deeply, because she never ever encouraged such cruel behavior. BB don't support or appreciate any man who beats a woman more so his wife. It is unmitigated, out-and-out gross, wicked and disrespectful not only to his wife but also to his children. She wept nightly as she watched the cycle of pain and abuse unfolding in her children.

This type of irrational conduct grieved her profoundly until once again she cried out to God in her distress asking when will this generational curse be broken?' Will the abuse ever end? Why was life so hard for her and her family? There BB was not yet healed from her brokenness and was being faced with her children's dilemma she tried talking to her abusive son but he refused to listen. In the midst of all this, his wife never left his side. Through BB's prayers, over the years just before his unfortunate death, she watched her son life gradually changed for the better.

About three years later, Jabez began to complain again with serious headaches and other complications. Within months, his health began to deteriorate. During that time, he opened up to one of his cousins for the first time in his life and talked about his childhood experiences and how it affected him. He talked about his job and the stress it was giving because of the low wages which was insufficient to support his family. He talked about the brutality of his sister by the hands of her father Jas someone whom he supposed to love and care for. He talked about his mother

BB's twenty-one years of abuse from his father which caused the family's separation and having them to flee to different countries. It was strange. He had everything bottled inside.

Three days after releasing his pent-up feelings to one of his family members, he fell ill and died. This tragedy took place three days after his thirty- third birthday leaving behind his wife and three small children. Now, BB have lost her two sons, one to substance abuse and one to the dust of the earth. The profound emptiness she felt was and still is unbearable. All she asked of God to please keep her safe as she grieve, sought answers to questions, raged and wept. Sometimes she sits in silence waiting to be heal and feel whole and alive again. Even in those moments, she knew God was with her. She felt His presence.

One thing BB has learnt from all of this, is that you cannot question God. He Knows what is best and He knew what He was doing. He promised in His word that He will not put any more on His children than they can bear. BB is now living by His promises because God is a God that does not lie. Now, she prays that God will continue to send his guiding angels to watch over Jabez family and keep them safe from all harm and danger.

All BB's children grew up thinking that she never loved them but it was not so. How could she explain to them that she does love them more than anything. All they wanted from her was the boldness and courage to say to them, she loves you guys and sacrifice herself to show her love. They wanted to see tough love that would have kept them going twenty-four hours a day, seven days a week and three hundred and sixty-five days a year. Lids did work hard to restore this tough love but could not because of her emotional stress.

As a family they had no social life. Her children's parenting was interrupted by other evil forces. She tried to instill in them that abuse is not a life sentence. There is still hope, healing and a chance to recover the self-lost in their childhood. So far, God had allowed her to see this light kindling in her son before his death. She paused to say 'Thank You God for that ray of light.

In BB's conclusion, she is writing to all parents everywhere, develop a good structure for your family with a loving and supportive relationship. When God is at the head, your family will feel safe, protected, respected, acknowledged and understood and that peace and harmony coexist with respect and interdependence. Communicate with them. Tell them you love them over and over again. Show them you love them, keep them safe from the ills of this world. Do not let the ills of society destroy them. Always remember that safe families are the foundation of a safe society. Blessed be the name of the Lord. BB is never going to give up on her children for as long as there is life there is hope. Prayers answered all things.

God promise BB, Zed, Jabez and Beth that He will give unto them beauty for ashes, the oil of joy for mourning, the garment of praise for the spirit of heaviness; that they might be called "Trees of Righteousness", the planting of the Lord, that he might be glorified (Isaiah 61:3. KJV). He further states that nothing bad will happen to us. No disaster will come to our home. For He has put His angels in charge of us. They will watch over us wherever I go. He said, if someone loves me, He will save them. (Psalm 91:10-11;14 NIV).

CHAPTER 6

NO OTHER WAY OUT (Divorce)

The Bible teaches: When a man takes a vow to the Lord or takes an oath to obligate himself by a pledge, he must not break his word but must do everything he said. (Numbers 30: 2)

Why could this not remain true for BB? What have she done that was so wrong that she had to break her vows to God? These questions deposited themselves into her head for a while.

After twenty-one years of living in an abusive marriage, BB saw no other way out but to flee for her life. Running away was all that she had known. She learned then, that the more she ran, the more she hurts. The growing pains that she tried so hard to escape throughout her marriage, drove her deeper and deeper into darkness. She was forewarned of the impending storm but as always, did not take heed.

She was faced head on with a Goliath-size problem. She did not know which way to respond. The forces of Jas were too big for her but she got the assurance that one day the Lord is going to save her from the claws of the lions and the bears and that God will indeed be with her. All she needed to do stay out of the devil's orchard.

Suddenly, she began to take an inventory of her life. Fleeing provided time for her to examine the Biblical principles on marriage and divorce. It gave her time to survey her strengths and her weaknesses. Even though the move removed her from the constant pressure of abuse and conflict, it still did not solve her problems. She was still carrying them around like heavy suitcases. As she reflected on past events of her life, she began to moan and groan prayerfully these words here I am again Lord, I have a problem I just cannot solve. I don't mean to worry you but I am facing something new and I need an answer that only you can give so, please answer me Lord.

BB began to ask God, what He wants her to understand from the situation that was haunting her. During that time her problems were insurmountable and it really frightened her. Her head felt as if she had worn a plaited crown of thorns with one piercing the dark aching muscles in the center of her brain. One that she could not figure out and could not get out of. Her hands and her body were crushed with torture. She felt soiled all over with mud and dirt just waiting to be cleaned up and dressed in an apparel of pure white. The pains in her body, was stagnant waiting to be swept away. She felt heavy and overloaded with the scum from the earth. She tried and tried to solve her disasters on her own but that did not work.

The battles were too great. BB could not continue that way. God had rescued her more times than she could count, but, her mustard seed faith kept weakening she was unable to say to her mountain be thou removed. Again she began to commune with the Master by turning the issue over to Him asking please do not get tired of her. Divorce is weighing heavily on her mind and she do not know if that was the right choice. She further stated, if it meets His approval to please show her a sign. She really needed to hear from Him to point her in the right direction. "Now, Lord you take over" she said. He was the Controller and the Supreme director of her dramatic life. She wanted Him to take charge and free her. BB was tired of making two steps forward and five steps backwards.

She had reached a fork in the middle of the road. She felt like the odds were stacked against her. She was struggling with a past filled with emotional starvation and injuries. BB had no alternative but to give up. There was no stable source to go to so, she turned to the one and only true source she knew, which is the Bible which drew her to many Scriptures concerning her issues. At that time, she did not know that there was a Scripture for every situation in one's life, until one day whilst doing a research, she came across Isaiah 41:13 which reads: "For I the Lord your God, will hold your right hand, saying to you, 'Fear not, I will help you'. That was her comfort, but had she known then? No! She knew God did not want her to live that way. He wanted her to be happy. He did not want her drifting along from place to place looking over the fence for greener pastures.

God had given BB this promise that, He will never leave her nor forsake her but will be with her until the end'. He continued by saying, I will not fail you either, for this battle is not yours but mine. So, Lids made up her mind to break free from the harmful life patterns. All of her desire was lost to fight again for a marriage that kept on going failing. she finally found true meaning in St. Paul's statement, 'I can do all things through Christ who strengthens me'.

After gaining her strength and courage, BB told her children of her plans to divorce their father with the hope that they will adjust. To her surprise, they happily agreed with the decision made. All they were concerned about was her happiness and for her to live a peaceful life so, she finally did it. The divorce proceedings began. It was a long and agonizing two-year experience. Jas did not contest it. He just refused to attend any of the court sessions. He ignored all of the telephone calls made to him by the lawyer. He evaded his responsibilities in all of that. BB was like the cheese standing alone. With the many puzzling and heart-wrecking questions from the judge, made her feel like surgery was being done on her brain with a blunt instrument.

The most important items on her agenda was her life, the spared embarrassment and safety of her children. Soon, the one-woman show and conflict was over leaving her in a financial confinement. It was a dead end experience with a deep pothole. It placed her in an antagonistic position and forced her to look after her own personal interest but it was finally over. Or was it really? Even though the cloud was moving through very slowly, one thing BB discovered, that her God was working behind the scenes for her all time. He was building a road beyond the dead end signs. Her call was, to believe in His promises and wait until He joins the roads and change her dead-end to a 'New Thing' in her life. God moves in a radical and mysterious way. He was closing that chapter in her life to open new ones. He assured her that each torturous ordeal was a cloud lined with silver. Each mangled trial was a miracle of lessons learned and wisdom about 'Be ye not unequally yoked together with unbelievers'. This is a teaching tool for all Christian women.

Another thing BB have learned that God never takes away something from her without giving her something in return. That is the God she serves. He is the God of her hurt. The God who brought her comfort and peace in the time of her confusion and sorrow. He was preparing her for a brighter tomorrow.

On the fifteenth day of June nineteen ninety-five, a sigh of relief breathed over BB, she finally signed her last document, therefore, ending that part of her life forever. Many at that time thought she could have beaten the odds and still try to make the travesty of her marriage work by saying to her God says you must forgive your brother seven times seventy, boy what a laugh! She had not laughed that way for a while. Her response was, 'Thank God I am free. I have done my part because I have exceeded my seven times seventy'. Maybe they were right but her life was more important. She believed in prayer and it still changes things. No matter what kind of upset she now encounters in her life, she will forever see this as a shift toward something bigger, better and greater.

It was then, BB decided not to waste another moment brooding and feeling sorry for herself for the Psalmist David taught her how to number her days aright that she may gain a heart of wisdom. These words were saying to her that life is too short and she must use the little time she has left wisely and for her eternal good. It explained that she should number her days by asking, 'What does she wants to see happen in her life now? What steps must she take toward that purpose? Whose report will she believe? Her in-laws and family, her personal family, the community or the report of the Lord? BB chose to believe the report of the Lord.

However, this separation brought BB a sense of emotional peace for that period of time. It stimulated a depth of openness in her communication that was absent from her life. She decided to 'Let go and let God' by making a fresh start with an enthusiastic zeal, set new goals for her future by burying herself in work to maintain her sanity and to support herself. She reverted to her old hobbies in expanding her creative abilities in acting, singing in the choir of her local church, crocheting, writing poems and drama scenes.

It was then, BB began to see a beam of light peeping through her dark clouds. She moved toward a personal recovery by establishing a stronger relationship with God. Even though the community shun divorce women this did not bother her, for, she knew the Lord was on her side. This still remains a problem today in society. Divorce women to them are being classified as 'Damaged Goods' or 'Corrupt Commodities'. To them there are no easy solutions to life after divorce but who made them judge and jury? For the Bible says, God is a God of order and not a God of confusion, fear anger violence and abuse.

In ancient times, Moses allowed divorce. Even though It was never condoned or encouraged by God, He still did not want to see his children being trapped in a marriage and being abused constantly, physically, mentally, spiritually or emotionally. We all should be sensible adults. The question is do you think God ever wanted BB to Stay in an abusive marriage? No way! The Lord did not expect or want her to suffer mental or bodily harm at the hands of her husband who is supposed to sacrificially love her. God did not want her to be oppressed or impaired by fear. Paul in 1 Corinthians 7:15, says in not so many words, any woman who is physically harmed or verbally belittled, insulted, or harassed by her spouse is under bondage and controls her mind and activities with threats or brutality is enslaving her.

Jesus came for the purpose of healing BB's broken heart, deliver her captives, and liberate her who was bruised. This perfectly describes BB's condition of someone who is being abused in her marriage. Jesus came to rescue her from that abusive relationships. Her leaving only happened when her spouse did violence to his house. Therefore, BB did not abandon her relationship. She challenged any and every one if you are in an abusive marriage or relationship do your best to get support for yourself, be willing to take the time to work through the Biblical process, and stay on your knees with God throughout the process, for a change. This will help make you the person God desires you to be. God is faithful and He does work all things together for good for those who love Him.

No matter what anyone thinks or says Jesus was and still is the answer. Like Isaiah, BB had labored. She was spending her life in vain and for nothing. Like David, she sought and called upon the Lord, to her God she cried for help. From His Throne He heard her voice and her cries to Him reached His ears and He saved her from all her troubles. When everyone had forsaken her the Lord took her in. This, friends and readers, were BB's "Only Way Out". When problems, trials and troubles get you down do not take matters in your own hands, try Jesus, it works.

CHAPTER 7

HIDING BEHIND THE MASK (Work)

Be eager to give them your best, serve them as you would serve Christ. Don't work hard only when your master is watching and then shirk when he isn't looking; work hard and with gladness all the time, as though working for Christ, doing the will of God with all your heart. (Ephesians 6:5-7).

This passage of scripture rang true for BB. Being a teacher, was very rough and tough during her crisis. Day after day, she would drag along all battered and bruised from the continuous beatings and in tremendous pain, to her work place. There were times she would lugged along in faith, with the assurance that one fine day, God is going to set her free. For He said in his Word: "Faith is the essence of things hoped for and the evidence of things not seen." She knew then, that faith was the only ingredient to her bright and happy future. So she held on to that verse.

Being all black and blue, BB had to stand in front of her classes with about twenty to thirty-three students ages ranging from ten plus to seventeen years old to teach. Despite the pain, she would brisk myself with smiles and teach to the best of her ability without the students recognizing her suffering. Again, she stepped out in faith knowing that God was on her side leading her and guiding her through that rough time. Just as the sessions ended, she would go into the bathroom in the quietness to tend her wounds and groan in prayer to God for His healing touch.

As time passed by, BB flesh began to waste away, her clothes began to sag and her voice began to squeak. It was as if a lump was in her throat blocking the food from going down, the little that she ate. BB's faith weakened and she became afraid not knowing what to do. She visited numerous doctors. One said it was stress, the other said it was her nerves, another voiced it was an ulcer, a fourth said it was grief. What really was it? She still did not know but was treated for them all with no positive results.

All of BB's problems were bottled up inside. She felt that keeping them inside seemed worst. The weight of it was tearing her up and holding her captive. She felt like she was standing on the edge of a cliff ready to jump. She then realized the time had come for her to review and re-examine herself and open up to someone and let them know what was going on inside of her and talk about the inward pain and suffering she was experiencing.

But who was that someone and where should that someone be? Is it possible to be able to confide in any of her co-workers? Would they understand BB's martyrdom, her crucifixion and coached her through it? Or would they gloat and use it as a weapon against her? Was she truly ready for this turn of event? These and numerous other questions whiz through her mind. Even though they were silent questions, deep down, she knew that God had already known the answers.

Carefully, BB began her search. Daily she began to scrutinized and test her co-workers at school. She started her testing by dropping little hints here and there. For example, whenever she heard a conversation about marriages or dating, she would jokingly say, 'Oh they all would beat you black and blue one day'; 'Make sure you look carefully before you leap'; Or "they may come to you like sheep in wolf's clothing'. Another hint she dropped was, 'Not all beds are made of beautiful roses, some are filled with thorns and some have thorns amongst the roses, so make sure in your searching do it really good. However, that did not work.

My next step was, to study them to see if she could find if only one who is trustworthy to share her troubles with. She decided to give it a try. This made her feel a little better, but soon after, BB found out the hard way. It was a mistake. She began hearing bits and pieces of the conversation here and there. She would walk in on little groups whispering and as soon as she approached them, the mutterings ceased. As she passed by, she could feel eyes all over her as if they were searching for something.

Then came the verbal abuse. BB was teased and made fun of in a supposedly joking manner. It was like knives piercing through her heart and thrusting in her back. She did not create a scene but smiled and walked away unnoticed and wept feeling betrayed and disappointed. She became too sensitive in her dealings with relatives and her associates. After all of this, she began regarding every adverse word as a criticism or an insult. This made her withdrawn from them all. All she wanted was a little love and consideration from her colleagues to relieve her of some of the fear of her estranged husband. Also to rid herself from the shadow of darkness lurking inside of her.

What BB was frantically searching for, was that one person who would believe in her to comfort and help her find a balm for her woe. One that, as she poured out her heart, would see their face filled with awe, their lips trembling and their eyes watering equally to her own. It was a bitter pill to swallow. God's Word states, love your enemies and pray for those who despitefully use you and in so doing, will heap coals of fire upon their head. So she retreated to the safety net of God's arms.

After drying her tears and washing her face, BB boldly stepped out of her hiding place asking the Lord to order her steps in His Word. David, when he was going through his troubles cried out to the Lord and said, "Though I walk in the midst of trouble, thou wilt revive me: thou shalt stretch thine hand against the wrath of mine enemies and thy right hand shall save me." (Psalms 138: 7). Then the words of Paul spoke and said: Sister "Be careful for nothing, but in everything by prayer and supplication with thanksgiving let your request be made known unto God".

At the very beginning, BB observed that, that little mole hill was turning into a mountain. She promised herself that she was not going to let that happen. She was not going to take on any added stress. Nor was she going to fret herself over evil doers. The truth of the matter was they were unethical, unprincipled and dishonest. BB was not going to let her colleagues and the world which surround her squeeze her into their own mold of deceitfulness. She was not going to copy the behavior and customs of this world, but let God transform her into a new person by changing the way she thinks. Then BB will know what God wants her to do and she will know how good, pleasing and perfect His will really is.

In the stillness of the day, the Lord whispered to her I have commanded thee over and over be strong and of a good courage, be not afraid neither be thou dismayed for I the Lord thy God is with thee whithersoever thou go. During that time, BB recognized that many of her teammates were not Christians so her last choice was put her trust in the Lord with all her heart and lean not unto her own understanding but in all her ways acknowledge Him and He will direct her paths.

BB did just that. She turned away from her circumstances for a while and turned into a work–a-holic, laughing, joking and 'Hiding Behind the Mask' of abuse as if everything was just fine and dandy. She continued to work in that unfriendly and uninviting atmosphere for a very long time. She had no genuine friends only a few acquaintances.

A few years later after being beaten so badly, she left leaving her career and everything behind. It was time to shift gears. No matter how difficult, challenging or hard it did seem, BB understood that shifts are necessary when the time comes to free oneself from the confinement of mental, emotional, and physical boxes of barbarism. BB changed schools.

After changing schools, she began to pick the problematic of trust apart piece by piece, until she got to the core. The answer was there facing her all the while which was Jesus. It was through his eyes her help will come. So, BB began this time with the help of the Lord searching again for an earthly true and honest friend. She knew there had to be one amongst that group because they appeared to be completely different from her last colleagues. This however took some time. Years later, she found one. She was a foreigner. Before she had a chance to approach her, she found her. As she approached BB, she blurted out I have been watching you from a distance. I discerned that you are going through a lot of pain and recognized your hurt. I even saw it in your smiles and hear it in some of your jokes, come and talk to me. Her name was Atufa Best meaning Kind and merciful.

Examining Atufa all over, BB started to refuse but froze. Sensing BB reluctance to continue, she interrupted and said you can talk to me. From her facial expression, BB saw she was sincere. Immediately, BB felt a wave of air blew over her. It was different. She was different. They both went into a quiet room where they would not be interrupted. BB began to open up to her. She revealed to her about her years of abuse and how she got there. She showed her the scars imprinted on her body from the numerous of beatings and bites. Her colleague listened with teary eyes as she related only a few of her dilemmas. She then gave BB a few words of encouragement and prayed with her.

Many days they prayed and talked about the promises of God's together. BB did not want the fellowship of togetherness to end. Her colleague was a Christian and had a close and personal relationship with God. She became that honest and true friend BB was longing for. That made her feel better.

BB's prayers were answered. God had given her that opportunity to gain a hold on her life through the plenty she gave for not fighting back and by waiting on His time. He had helped her gain the satisfaction for a job well done. He was saying to her concentrate on pleasing me rather than trying to gain favor from those around you. From then on, God has placed 'Favor' on her life through that guardian angel. Even though she is no longer with BB, she still can hear her prayers and her words of wisdom ringing in her ears and resting upon my heart daily.

Atufa always reminded BB that God is her refuge and strength a very present help in times of trouble. She also told BB that God promise not to put any more on His children than they can bear and that she, BB has to go through the valley in order to reach her mountain. BB began to laugh more often. She crept out of her shell. There was a change in her life. She began to do her job better and produced better results from her students. Thanks be to God and Atufa.

During that phase of her life, BB got divorce. There was nothing to hold on to but her faith for the abuse was a problem she just could not control or solved. Now, she was not going to let the past hurts strangled or choked her anymore. She was not going to be defeated. BB sought suggestive methods to maintain a stable state of mind. Most importantly, she kept on fighting letting nothing shake her faith in God. BB kept moving forward and kept on striving. Because of that, God had definitely moved her out of that phase of her life.

BB no longer hid behind the mask of physical cruelty. Her mood changed from a sense of utter failure to a sense of blessed joy which spelt R-E-L-I-E-F and G-O-D who listened, helped and delivered her. One thing she had learned was that she must always believe in herself. All she had to do was take the sour lemon that was thrown at her and add the ice cubes that everyone had tossed at her and make it into sweet lemonade rather than bathing herself in the sour lime juice. BB now know that life will never play fair, not only for her, but for no one. There are still going to be times when life is going to hurl some curve balls but all she needs to do is be prepared.

In BB's final analysis, she realized that to fight her abusive tormentor depended on two things:

1) whether she was going to sit around and get enraged at life or

2) do her job the best she knew how.

BB chose number two with the confidence that she was working for God's glory and not for man or her own. She also acknowledged that she was working towards a common goal to educate a generation and with the surety that those she worked with will see Jesus shining in and through her and be brought closer to Him. Then and only then, she decided to give of her best and loyal devotion to the Master into the battle for truth. Clad in salvation's full armor by giving Him first place in Her service consecrating every part.

CHAPTER 8

BURNED BUT NOT CONSUMED

The Lord shall guide thee continually and satisfy thy soul in drought and make fast thy bones, and thou shall be like a watered garden, and like a spring of water whose waters fail not. (Isaiah 55:11).

After being treated so shabbily, during BB's divorce, she had no breathing space. She plunged directly into a legal battle which entailed many complications related to finances and personal issues. The muck and mire grew so thick, she felt as if the walls were closing in on her again. Many days, she woke up to empty cupboards finding it hard to make ends meet all by herself. BB, soon discovered that the end of her marriage was the beginning of a new financial crisis. When will it ever end she wondered.

There were days when BB had nothing left to hold on to. There were times she felt like Moses and the Israelites travelling through the dry and dusty desert in search for food and longing for some manna to rain down for her from heaven. No matter how hard she tried, she could never manage to save a penny. That was her dry season. BB financial output exceeded her financial income.

She felt like a banana when it left its bunch and got skinned. She felt as if she was going insane not knowing which way was up.

From week to week, month to month, BB would watch people doing their grocery shopping. She had a deep feeling that God wanted her to know that He is her Alpha and Omega her beginning and her end. He was her Jehovah-Jireh her provider and promised in His word that He would take care of her. He declared that He is the supplier of all her needs according to his riches in glory through his son Jesus.

When BB's ancillary relief proceedings got started, things became very ugly and more tough for her. She was left to face them alone. A timetable was requested by the court for the exchange of information and documentation in preparation for trial. BB made a list of her most important concerns arising out of her pending divorce. The issues at hand then were physical and mental abuse, housing and property settlements among other issues. In relationship to the welfare of her family, they were all grown therefore leaving her with no dependents, so that issue was null and void.

BB spouse did not show up for any of the court proceedings. She was left to paddle her own canoe among the rough waves. It got more and more stressful each time. She was bombarded with puzzling head-splitting questions with words, phrases and sentences she have never heard of. She guessed they were lawyer's terms. Being an educator this made her looked like a dummy. The intense battles were housing and property settlement. She felt as if the lawyer was bias. Why couldn't he exercise his legal powers and demand that her spouse attended his court sessions? Instead, he grilled her until she began to char.

Tackling this exigent resource was war. There was no working together, no planning, no direct communication but relayed obscene messages, warnings and frets. What better therapy there would have been if only he would just come and faced the problems as a sane adult but instead, he acted like a coward. Feeling troubled, BB meditated on these words wait on God, keep His ways and He will exalt her and He would see to it that the wicked is cut off. Due to the intense drill by the lawyer no progress was being made nor was BB understanding anything so, she changed lawyers. This change opened her eyes to a much more understandable procedure.

The frequent visits to the lawyer's office gave BB some insights on how to go about making this puzzle a little easier. The lawyer highlighted some really good points that he thought would get things under control without throwing stones back and forth at each other. The forces BB was up against pushed her to put her newborn eighteen – month old house with everything in it up for sale. She saw no other way out.

Within this problem, another one arose. BB's spouse remained in the home without paying his share of mortgage and refused to meet the sworn agreement made and signed by him, to share the liabilities allocated through the divorce court, thus, leaving her to shoulder all the responsibilities financially. She was the only contributor to the mortgage which was the most significant part of her monthly payment.

BB's spouse upon hearing that she had placed the home on the market for sale, became irrational and demented. He threatened many buyers and scared them away. This fight lasted for about three long years. In the meantime, the lawyer's fee kept increasing. Losing faith, she began to blame God because He promised to supply all of her needs. He promised to be there for her in good times and in bad. Where was He? Ever a time she needed Him was then. Deep inside, BB knew she was being selfish and ungrateful because God had just brought her out of two terrible and vicious attacks, domestic abuse and divorce, now, there she was grumbling and complaining. Boy Oh boy! Thank God He is not like man and He is a forgiving God.

The situation at hand began to worsened. It was like arrows and darts coming at her piercing her from every direction. She had to deal with two forces, his family and him. That experience was not like any other BB had ever encountered before. It made her weak very weak. She felt like surrendering, throwing in the towel for the mortgage was too high and too heavy a load for her to carry all by herself, plus to allow Jas to live in a house she was paying for.

Due to BB's insecurities and betrayal, things became a nightmare. Some nights, she would just lay there thinking to the point where her head throbbed until she became nauseated. The physical pain was almost unbearable and the emotional pain was even worse. BB began to hear voices inside her head saying, 'Go get them child! Fight back with your hidden weapons you refuse to let out'. It was the devil speaking. At that moment, hatred crept in. The walls were closing in. BB became desperate and vicious because desperate times then called for desperate measures. After doubting God, she began lashing out at everyone and everything in my path. She made a drastic change and began taking matters into her own hands and doing things her way. She was at the end of her rope. She turned into an unidentified monster.

Within seconds, the flesh that was left on her body continue to fall away even more. BB felt as light as a feather. Her eating habits were very poor. Was she still saved? Yes! At that time her problems seemed bigger than God, so she thought, and they were taking her down the wrong direction. Her road was paved with multiple lanes confusing her. She could not find the right exit.

The day came, when BB was too weak to move a muscle, out of the blue she cried out to God again. It was fright that made her do it. She cried convulsively in prayer, God ever a time BB needs you is now'. Do not leave her hanging at the edge of this treacherous cliff alone. She has no strength left to hold on. It is too steep for her and much too dangerous. Her hands are bruised and blistered and she is soiled all over inside and out. Please dear God free her in Jesus name. BB continued cast her not away from thy presence oh Lord! Take not thy Holy Spirit from her, restore unto her the joy His salvation and uphold her with thy free Spirit (Psalm 51:10–12). Lord she continued, she has turned into someone she doesn't know please bring her back to that place where she first believed in Jesus name Amen!

In BB's anguish she cried out but things grew from bad to worse. Again she began visiting several doctors for a condition she was in with no balm and no medicine seemed to cure the mysterious illness. One day after crawling here and there, BB began ripping apart the events that had her bound. There she was searching to see where her down fall lie. She began turning the situation inside and out to get to the core of the problem, then a thought rang clear BB you have not asked God for His forgiveness, oh ye of little faith. Suddenly, it felt like an arrow had pierced through her heart without a warning. That was the answer to the questions which clogged her mind. It was right there all the time locked up in her head. It was what she was seeking for.

Immediately, BB fell prostrate on her face before the Lord pleading, begging for His forgiveness and allowed Him to take over her issues. She once came across a slogan which read: 'Instead of telling God how big your problems are, tell your problems how big God is'. She remembered it and took that advice. Lying there, she wept uncontrollably in silence for a while. She could not pray for there were no more words left. She was crying but without tears. She groaned mercilessly for God's forgiveness and asking for patience to wait like His Servant Job did in Biblical days.

During this encounter, BB felt a heavy load weighing about a ton being lifted off her shoulders, her vision became clearer and her heart began to beat at its normal pace. To sum it all up, like before she felt as if human hands were lifting her up only this time it was spiritual hands lifting her burdens away. Day by day, she began to see things in a different light. God began to work out a plan for her. His word was saying to her:

"For I know the plans I have for you, they are plans for good and not for disaster, to give you a future and a hope. When you pray, I will listen. If you look for me in honesty, you will find me when you seek me. I will end your captivity and restore your fortunes". (Jeremiah 29:11–14).

Soon after, the days became brighter and brighter for Lids. Just how God shut the mouths of the lions for Daniel so He did for BB when she was thrown into my enemy's territories. It was then she lifted up her eyes unto the Hills where help came from. The Lord became her light and her salvation therefore, she feared no evil. The Lord became the strength of her life she was not afraid any longer. When the wicked, even her enemies and her foes, came upon her to eat up her flesh, they all stumbled and fell. Though a host encamped against her, heart had no fear. Though war arose against her she was confident that no harm will come near her. For in the time of her troubles the Lord had once again came to her rescue and hid her in His pavilion in the secret of His tabernacle. He set her upon a rock and lifted her head above her false enemies, delivering her from them that surrounded her and rise up against her and breathed out cruelty. BB then offered up sacrifices of joy and sang praises unto the Lord.

Time continued to drag on but it was no bother to BB then again the Psalmist warned her that vengeance belongs to the Lord and He will show himself in time and so He did. She must not fret herself of evil doers, neither shall she be envious against them because they are workers of iniquity. He continued by saying, they would soon be cut down like the grass, and wither as the green herb and if BB trust in the Lord, and do good she will dwell in the land and be well fed.

Just when BB was about to forget about her financial problems, a call came concerning the sale of the home. The buyer said, despite her ex-husband rantings and ravings, he was determined more than ever to purchase the home. The process took a little longer than expected because of a few rough conflicts but, BB won in the end. God came through for her. BB continued to thank God and still thanking Him for her breakthrough. If it was not for the Lord on my side where would she be? Now as a part of BB's testimony she almost let go. She felt like she just couldn't take life anymore because her problems had her bound and depression weighed her down. The devil thought he had her but Jesus came and grabbed her. God's mercy kept her and He held her close and wouldn't let her go. BB is alive and here today because of God's grace and mercy.

The light became even more brighter in BB's life. Even though she was not fully compensated for the amount of effort and finance she placed into the marriage it was the least of her worries. One good thing about it all, there were no surrendered values on endowments or vehicles to discuss. BB just wanted that nightmare to be over. She did not want anything else to further complicate her life or to drag it on. After the settlement, it was revealed to her that, she must know that all things work together for good to them that love God and to them who are called according to his purpose. (Romans 8:28).

During that facet of BB's life, she learned many life lessons. The most important one was, and still is, that God is the source of her mercies, and He will never fail her. No heat, or drought can parch her sea. She was, back then, focusing on her problems rather than the solution. She listened to her heart for answers and watched for signs knowing quite well, money could not and would not ease her pain. BB also learned that God through His word has established laws of protection and provision from the seed to the farmer and that with Him all things are possible. She channeled all her attention to people who made her prosperity impossible.

The results of this episode took BB to a whole new dimension in my life. She began to pray daily to God for her needs to be met because her lessons taught her, that it is only through God, that she lived, moved and have her being. BB's prayer life began to grow stronger and stronger. Daily she asked God to keep her in His will and let her not be entangled ever again with the yoke of bondage or be unequally yoked together with unbelievers.

Another lesson learned, was that hardship can be overcome. They are a useful part of God's Master plan, His perspective, His preservation and His preparation. The suffering made BB recognized the importance of her existence. It was also unveiled to her in that she must not be deceived because God is not mocked, for whatsoever a man sow, he will also reap and that she must not be weary in doing well, for she will reap in due season, if she faints not.

He also showed BB that they that sow in tears shall reap in joy. This gave her the satisfaction of knowing that the day was fast approaching when the sun is really going to shine in a cloudless sky through her back door. All she needed to do was to lean and depend on Jesus because he was and is her only friend. The time then came for BB to empty herself of the abundance of anger, and make herself into something useful. Even though she was 'Burned, she was not consumed'.

BB's God fulfilled her beyond her asking with many surprises. She came before Him in her penitence, and He granted her the desires of her heart. He loaded her with benefits of love, peace, joy and contentment. He made BB joint-heir with Jesus His son and allowed her to have access to the riches of heaven. She became ashamed, for she had lived far below what God had provided for her. God was never lacking and never late in her life. He allowed BB to open her eyes, and see the showers of His abundant riches He is showering on those who opened the doors of their mind with trust, faith, praise and a solid budget which includes giving, sharing and receiving. He was telling her that it is in Him she had an unending supply of hope in the midst of her uncertainty and that Godliness with contentment is great gain. For we brought nothing in this world and it is certain we are not going to carry anything out.

BB learned that God is able to do abundantly all that we ask or think and that He is able to make all grace abound toward us, that is always having all sufficiency in all things. So, BB decided to obey and serve God with all her heart, soul and body so that the rest of her days can be spent in prosperity. Her life can now be used to enrich the lives of others around her.

God showed BB how to respond to financial attacks in her life. He educated her how to sow extra financial seeds by faith with confidence, expecting it to break the strangled – hold that was on her finances. He indoctrinated in her that she must take no thought, what she shall eat, drink or be clothed, for He knew that she had need of all these things. He wanted her to seek Him first, His kingdom and His righteousness and all things will be added unto her and whatsoever she shall ask in His name, that will He grant. Jesus said that He is the 'The Bread of Life', and He will satisfy BB's thirst. So, why was she searching everywhere for help knowing quite well her help was coming from the Lord.

After going through that dry season, it awakened BB to this revelation that, the day she was born again in Christ, was the richest day of her life. It was the day she became filthy rich with Jesus Christ as her Lord and Savior. It was the day she obtained the legal right to claim all of the promises of God. Why was she settling for something less when God, was allowing her to drink from His living water? From all of this, BB has discovered that the disappointments in her life were simply the hidden appointments of God's love, mercy, grace and His prosperity. Here she was again 'Burned but not Consumed'.

In my final dissection on this chapter, to those of you who are experiencing the same financial havoc in your life, read God's word there is enough assuring scriptures there to help everyone overcome their problems. Scriptures that would help ease your heavy load. They have all the answers you need that can turn every situation around into one of love, happiness and prosperity. Just read, have faith, believe and put your trust in Him and He will see you through. Here is something BB is leaving with you that has blessed her life tremendously.

The 23rd Psalm along with its explanations in a nutshell:

The Lord is my Shepherd .... Relationship.

I shall not want .... Supply.

He maketh me to lie down in green pastures .... Rest.

He leadeth me beside the still waters .... Refreshment.

He restoreth my soul .... Healing.

He leadeth me in the path of righteousness .... Guidance.

For his name sake .... Purpose.

Yea though I walk through the valley of the shadow of death...

....Testing.

I will fear no evil .... Protection.

For Thou art with me .... Faithfulness.

Thy rod and thy staff they comfort me .... Discipline.

Thou prepares a table before me in the presence of enemies......

.... Hope.

Thou anointest my head with oil .... Consecration.

My cup runneth over .... Abundance.

Surely goodness and mercy shall follow me all the days of my life

.... Blessings.

And I shall dwell in the house of the Lord .... Security.

Forever and ever Amen! .... Eternity.

Now, BB is thanking God every day for allowing her to have access to His riches in heaven. May God continue to bless all of you richly. As you can now see that even though 'BURNED, BB was NOT CONSUMED.

CHAPTER 9

THE TURNING POINT

"I will build you using fairness. You will be safe from those who would hurt you, so you will have nothing to fear. Nothing will come to make you afraid, I will not send anyone to attack you. So no weapon that is used against you will defeat you. You will show that those who speak against you are wrong. These are good things my servants receive. Their victory comes from me" says the Lord. (Isaiah 54:14, 17 NIV).

BB faith then looked up to God the Lamb of Calvary. He heard her when she prayed and washed all of her guilt away. Where there was hatred, doubt, despair, darkness and sadness in her life, He sowed love, faith, hope, light and joy. He gave her rest from her sorrows, fear and from the hand of bondage.

BB's life was filled with personal storms and challenges. Her emotional and physical storms were unbearable and devastating with a ton of nature's volcanoes and tornadoes. Carefully, she began to flip through the pages of her life and searched its contents. She meditated on every boisterous wind that blew, every frightening clap of thunder that roared and every fork of fierce lightning that took her picture as it lit up the sky and every part of her body. During that time, the thick scab from the horrific storms began to remove a layer at a time from her eyes allowing a narrow shaft of light to shine through. It made her realized, then that no thorns will be able to prick her even if she leaned against them again.

In not so many words, its contents were saying, that it is BB's God-given privilege to live in a happy and fear-free community and deserve to be treated with dignity and respect. In addition, she should never let contretemps get her down except on her knees. James 5:16 says: If there is any among you suffering, they should keep on praying about it. In retrospect, BB understood her life. She was so busy adding up her troubles that she had forgotten to count the blessings God was showering her with.

Isaiah taught BB that she must wait on the Lord and she will find new strength. She will fly high on wings like eagles. She will run and not grow weary, she will walk and not faint. He was instructing her to have patience, faith and courage because this trio is like a kite where the peaceful wind raises it higher to a new and smoother level.

BB held on knowing that God would mend broken hurts and give everyone a brand new start whoever believes in Him. He was assuring BB in a variety of ways that He has good things in store for her. He has plans for peace and not of hurt. He has intentions of prosperity and not suffering. He has plans to make her happy and not to harm her. God in all of this had her welfare in mind. To sum it all up, God's plans for her was not failure, misery, poverty, sickness, or disease but to have a wonderful life full of good health, happiness, and fulfillment.

These plans gave BB so much to look forward to. She discovered, she had so much to live for. This time, she was not going to allowed the devil to steal her joy. Suddenly, she saw her sufferings with a light of perseverance. Now, through her trials, she has found character and confidence knowing that she has God's eternal hope not ever to remember the former things neither to consider the things of old. The Lord is now doing a 'New thing in her life.

After stumbling upon all of this, BB escaped to a brand new territory where ninety-percent of its population was new to her. She knew then that God had created her to want a 'New beginning'. She felt this move was a step in the right direction. It was a direction where new things began about to happened. God knew she needed help in understanding His plan for her life so He sent His Holy Spirit as her Guide, her Teacher, her Counselor, her Deliverer, her Comforter her Advocate, her Helper and her Intercessor. As she began to trust the Holy Spirit that was dwelling in her, she gradually became everything God had planned for her to be. Whatever was troubling her, she shook it off without fear and trembling. BB's dreams for a bright and prosperous future, left no room for any more serpent bites. She now placed her faith and trust in God and He gave her the strength to stand and accomplish whatever He asks of her.

BB's move took place during her summer vacation period which led her to another phase in her life. Her job became the first important factor. She was being faced with a decision. It was a tough one. She had to decide whether or not to ask for a transfer or go back living in 'Hell on earth after God had revealed His plans for her life. But being a firm believer in God, the Holy Spirit instructed her to ask for the transfer. Humbly, she presented her case to her authorities along with her application. They sympathetically understood her plight and granted her request. Even though it was not where she wanted to be, it still made her very happy and she accepted the offer. It was a place at one of the Primary Schools for there were three.

The day came when BB had to report to duty. Shyness came over her not because of the new faces and new environment but because of the scar on her face. She began to wonder what would it be like seeing both teachers and students steering at her. Not really at her but at the scar on her face. Would they laugh, make fun, or accept her the way she is? Even though BB was an adult, these thoughts still crept up in her mind. Soon, she had learnt that her worries were all in vain. There she was for a brief moment allowing her mind and emotions to get the best of her over things she had no control over. She was again falling into Satan's trap of being negative but quickly, she fought back and chose to believe God and got ready to receive the wonderful blueprint He had drawn ahead for her. BB knew and felt that something good and wonderful was waiting for her. She then recognized that God had not given her a Spirit of fear and if fear ever comes knocking at the door and stepped on her heart again, she would send 'Faith' to open it. Hallelujah'.

The first day on her Job, she was given a class of twenty–four students to teach. Being a High school teacher for the most part of her teaching career, her work was cut out for her. This was not really new to her but it had been a very long time since she had taught at Primary school level but there are two sayings that she believed still rings true for her which say, 'Once a teacher always a teacher' and 'Success comes in cans and failure comes in cants'. But the most important saying that is above all the others was she can do all things through Christ who strengthens her.

Throughout that day she kept repeating this Scripture verse over and over and it gave her courage.

Each time BB puts her trust in God, the light in her life became brighter and brighter. There, she had met new and genuine acquaintances. She developed a good rapport with her students who esteemed and respected her highly. She felt as if she was walking on air. For a very long time in BB's life true happiness began to paved her life. However, like everything else this bliss only lasted for one school year.

Just as they were enjoying each other company, disappointment struck. BB was ripped away from her students and was transferred to the High School on the island. It was a moment of sadness not only for the students, but for the entire Primary School family especially the time when she had to say goodbye. She saw the tears and heard their pleas saying 'Don't go'. Her only comfort to them was, even though she will not be with them in person, they will be in her prayers and in her thoughts. Also, most of you will meet her again on your placement to the High School so, study hard and try to be the best you can be.

As days passed by, BB became more and more settled and more comfortable. This new feeling gave her the incentive to travel. She took up the challenge. During her first vacation in her newfound home, she was invited to travel to a Church Conference in Louisville Kentucky. This really was the "Turning Point' for her. She met a lot of Christian people. They laughed and sang together. The most amazing thing that happened on the trip was meeting a middle aged lady who was assigned as her and her group's bus driver. She became so fascinated with the sweet fellowship on the bus that every time she drove them she would request they sing for her. It was truly a blessing to BB to see how

God was using her along with others to bless someone through songs of praises and thanksgiving.

As they sang, BB envisioned her dark clouds disappearing one at a time allowing her bleak sky to grow clearer and clearer letting more and more light to penetrate through. One of her favorites was "I feel like traveling on, though storms may rise on every hand I feel like traveling on'. The song confirmed that her trials only came to make her strong and that weeping may endure for a night but joy comes in the morning. It was telling her to hold on. This brief moment of jubilation ended leaving a lasting impression on her mind.

BB's vacation ended. A new school year arrived. She was transferred back into another High School. The time came to face another new school body not only with new faces but also a new generation with a new attitude. Even though she was a little fearful, she didn't allow it to dominate her. BB boldly stepped into the gate wearing a smile of confidence which was her weapon of readiness and preparation for any darts that will be thrown at her. Again to her surprise nothing of that sort happened. Again she knew that God was really with her and in Him she placed her trust. He was her shield. School began and she was introduced. She felt a wave of relief when she looked around and saw a multitude of happy faces smiling at her. Within seconds, she felt wanted and accepted. The Lord is a faithful God. Blessed are those who wait for Him to help them.

It indicated that there is really a God upstairs who was waiting and longing for an opportunity to turn things around for BB and to show her His goodness. He is a God of Justice and is always ready and willing to correct her every wrong and her way of thinking. The only thing He required of her was to believe His promises. This also told her that God had never forgotten her because the Scriptures had proven to her that He is faithful and will not let her be tempted or mistreated beyond what she can bear. It also stated that God will always provide a way out of no way so that she can withstand any temptation which may block the entrance.

It is here where BB placed a full-stop at the end of this time in my life. She left the old bondage behind and took possession of her rightful place. She had grown tired of playing games with her life and doubting God when all the while He was helping her. She was tired of wearing different masks and pretending to be someone else other than herself. She began to see through her phantom. God's promises kept her stable until His timing came to illuminate her nightmares.

BB obeyed Timothy when he urged her to be calm, cool and steady. She chose to learn from hurtful experiences instead of allowing them to make her bitter. She began to overcome evil with good by making sure she did not hurt others the way she was hurt. BB refused to render evil for evil. This was a good time to wipe the slate clean and start a new chapter in her life. God causes everything to work together, for the good of those who love Him and are called according to His divine purpose and plan.

What else can BB say to these things but if God be for her who can be against her. She was hard pressed on every side and could not find her way out. She was caught up in the cycle of violence. She had to trudge through the confusing and embarrassing court system alone. She was mentally and physically abused from childhood to adulthood to womanhood and did not know what to do but thank God for His Word which instilled in her that He is faithful and He will provide a way for her. He did just that.

Thank You Lord for turning her life around. Because of this, all things are now working together and are fitting perfectly into God's plan for her life.

It was during this time in BB's life, she began writing poems to occupy her time and her mind. One day whilst reading a magazine, she stumbled across an advertisement from the 'International Society of Poets' asking for entries for a poetry competition. She jumped at the opportunity and entered. Her poem was entitled, 'My Mirror and I'. Surprisingly, it was selected from among hundreds of entries thus nominating her to be inducted as a 'Distinguished Member of the 'International Society of Poets in Washington D.C. What an honor!

Upon receiving this information, BB's tears began to flow like rain as she screamed with gratification and thanksgiving. The talent that was hidden inside her from a child began to come alive. That day all of her colleagues celebrated with her. The Principal and staff at her school all joined in and gave her a cash donation to assist with her trip to Washington D.C to receive her awards.

The day of traveling finally came. BB was accompanied by her oldest sister and an entrusted friend. When she entered the building where the ceremony was held, she almost collapsed when she saw the crowd. It was packed to capacity. Poets were everywhere from all over the world. There were not enough room to turn around. Elbows were rubbing against elbows. She was so thrilled to be socializing with other Christian poets – yes there were Christians poets there. They had a jovial time of togetherness. A memorable time. A time where there were not enough words in a thesaurus to describe it. Upon receiving her awards, BB felt like a Queen sitting on her throne not just an ordinary throne but God's Throne.

Whilst there, BB had the opportunity of meeting a few Stars like the old time famous singers 'The Platters' who graced their presence with songs of tranquility, relaxation and peacefulness. Then there was Montel Williams a host of a talk show and a few others were in attendance. She also had the pleasure of touring the country and saw 'The White House' the home of the President of the United States of America.

During her tour, BB's long - time dream of wishing to become a star had come true. She began to ask herself if this really real or, had she died and gone to heaven. She could not sit still. BB did not know how to act. In her wildest imagination, she never thought that life for her would or could be so sweet but, then again it was God who made it all possible. This was another one of God's plan for her life coming to pass.

Another chapter unveiled in BB's life was an acting career. Within months, she became a part of a drama club called 'FACES' a Christian non-profit organization. As a group they traveled to many churches and to one of the neighboring islands performing and blessing the hearts of many. The light in her life was sure glowing brighter and brighter as the days go by.

This move in BB's life had turned her dream into a reality. She became a star in her own rights. She became a star for Jesus. These were Gods' plans for her unfolding one by one, not her own. These experiences brought heavy drops of tears to her eyes but this time they were tears for rebuilding her self-worth, self-esteem, self-sufficiency, self- assurance, self-confidence, self-reliance, self-satisfaction and self-value that were stolen from her. Here is where her persistence paid off.

It was here God looked beyond BB's faults and saw her need and turned her life around for the good. It was because of her faithfulness and obedience to His Word that she is where she is today. Did she thank Him? Oh yes! she did, over and over again and still is as He continues to make her light shine before men.

CHAPTER 10

DAWN OF A NEW DAY

Behold! How good and pleasant it is for brethren to dwell together in unity. (Psalms133:1).

Lord Teach BB to come into Your presence with a contrite heart, and let her depart with the knowledge that her sins are forgiven. Fill her spirit with the peace which the world cannot give.

BB felt that the time had come for her to move into a new and better direction and a new phase in her life. So, she began to search for a church that will help her with her healing. After attending many churches, she finally found a Holy Ghost, Spirit – filled one where an anointed man of God, stands for truth and righteousness and one who is rooted and grounded in the Word of God. One who uses St. John 10:10 as the Church's foundation upon which it is being built.

After coming this far by faith, BB was not going to allow anyone or anybody shake her faith in God. She was destined not to let anyone or anybody cause her to misrepresent God's Word and His Church. She vowed to be a part of God's program and get her share of what God had for her because traumatic events left a void in her soul that only a closer relationship with God could filled. All she wanted and still do now more than ever is to be a walking Bible that many can read.

BB wanted to look beyond the valley of dry bones. She was not contented to rest in its mists. She knew that the summit of a Mountain awaited her. Why should she sit there with a saddened tear – stained face when she could be anointed with heavenly oil? Why should she suffer in a blackened dungeon, when opportunities are presenting itself to walk her on the roof of a fortress overlooking a rich lush landscape?

She allowed the Lord to rest His hand upon her in a brand new way. She permitted Him to pour the oil of His Holy Spirit deep into her veins and let the powerful fragrance be felt, sensed and seen by others who are near and dear to her. It definitely was moving time for her. BB decided to wake up from her lowly condition and make God the source and center of her soul by going to church and fellowship with other Christian believers. It was then, God began to open new doors for BB breaking the chains that had her bound. She was so overwhelmed with joy, that unexplainable feelings overtook her. BB felt like the writer, she wanted to scale the utmost height and catch a glimpse of God's glory bright. This was the beginning of a new experience for her, one that felt really good.

Whenever BB entered the doors of the church, she felt a warmth in her heart. The worship experience was so awesome, so rich in spirit that in an instant God's presence enveloped her placing her in an attitude of worship. Whatever her problems were, pain, grief and loses all disappeared. All she did was celebrate Jesus. Never ever was she so happy, happy in the Lord. This brought a ray of hope in her life. She began to accept herself for what she was. She was willing to put her best foot forward even if it was too big. BB prayed to God to help her to accept the things she could not change, courage to change the things she can and to grant her wisdom to know the difference.

This knowledge, prepared BB to face another new day, another week to go happily about her daily duties walking in victory. This also made her realize that she needed this balance in her life and to identify genuine believers who will share the weight of glory and not just its glamour. God was getting ready to send her some assistance that would help her to release whatever was bottled up inside of her. He gave BB the grace and the courage to finally close that portal and lead her towards a new entry waiting to be opened that will take her to the next step He prepared for her.

Another revelation that was revealed to BB during the sweet fellowship was, that, everything happens for a reason. God was saying to her that to everything there is a season, even in times of losses, disappointments, tears and sorrow. That was my season, a season of feeling bereft and lonely; confused and lost. God was watching over her all of the time because there was something inside of her so strong whispering, keep remembering that to everything there is a season. She noticed a faint glimmer of hope at the end of her long, narrow, dark, wet, cold tunnel of despair. The more she focused on the voice, the louder it became. The more she sought the light, the brighter it became. God heard her despairing cry to serve Him, so, He made her active in the church.

God surrounded BB with people who were kind, helpful and supportive. Christian people who understood her plight and felt her pain. BB began thanking Him daily for this breakthrough and for the extended Christian family He has blessed her with. She offered up thanks to Him daily for her adoption into that family where she was loved and loved unconditionally. Because of this, BB became an active, energetic kingdom builder not for herself, but for the glory of God and for the salvation of precious lost and hurting souls. As a result of this, she began to serve in the Outreach Department going in the community from door to door, praying, sharing the Word of God, giving gifts such as food, money and gospel tracks.

While doing this, BB discovered that she was living a religious life not really a Christian life. She didn't have a sense of purpose nor a sense of direction back then. All she was doing, burying herself deeper and deeper into her miseries. Upon this detection, she joined the choir, a choir that was going somewhere and on the march for Jesus. This was another one of childhood dreams coming to pass. Even though she was advance in years and the oldest member in the choir, that did not worry her the least. This move took her to another new level. God just kept on lifting her higher and higher. As a choir, she began touring various islands on fire for God singing, praising and worshipping under the anointing. During those road trips, many hearts were blessed.

These were happy moments for BB. She never knew that life could ever be so serene. God always comes through for us even when we think it is not possible, but Paul keeps on reminding us that with God All things are possible once we believe (Philippians 4:13). Shortly after, BB became a Sunday School's Superintendent. It helped her grow stronger and stronger not only in her Christian walk with God but also in His word. BB then lifted up her hands in praise saying, 'Lord if You can use anything You can use all of her, her hands, her feet, and her heart because she was available to Him. Her storage was completely empty. BB wanted the Spirit of the Living God to fall afresh on her. He wanted Him to mold, melt, break and fill her empty storage with His presence. She wanted Him to fall afresh on her.

BB had so much to give God thanks for. He delivered tomorrow's fears and today's anxieties that overload and blow all of the fuses. He had taken her through a Babylonian experience to obtain her blessings. The church became a powerful place to her with a powerful force. It was there, she took the mask off and finally came out of hiding. It was there she took the limits off God and believed in him. Now, she got her mind made up and she would not turn back. She reached the point in her life of no return. BB was running far too long away from God. Now, He is saying to her it's time to stop. So, she surrendered to Him and have invited Him not only into her heart, but her home and work place as well.

From that day forward, God continues to give BB strength for her body. He continued to fill her anew with His joy and love. God knew everything and has never made any mistakes. She felt Him every day feeding her. He never left her or forsaken her. He dealt with her situations in His own time because He is a God who is not slack concerning His promises. He has spoken to her through His Word and has shown her the way that she should go and warned her against the pitfalls of life. Through the church, God had given her the directives for her Christian living. It was because of her obedience to Him, He has open more and more gateways of opportunities and services for her. He gladly allowed her to enter and serve Him with the ability He had given her.

The newfound sweet fellowship BB enjoyed with her fellow saints, inspired her to let her light shine down until she shall see the light of God's glory up above. This newfound family had enabled her to render greater and greater service to her heavenly Father and to all she came into contact with. The Bishop in some of his sermons has also spoken into her life with words and phrases of encouragement which helped her more than he knows. Here are some of the pointers that was directed to her:

- Your moving time is a call from God.
- You must process all of the fruit of the spirit in order to make the journey.
- Take risks and step out in faith.
- Challenge your convictions.
- Stop using your weakness as an excuse or you will stay where you are.
- Make a declaration to press on to another level in Jesus Christ.

That is what BB did by saying to the Lord, she loved the habitation of His house and the place where His honor dwells. After hearing the powerful commands, BB is presently devoting her time mentoring, encouraging and helping others who are now experiencing the same dilemma.

BB is now walking worthy of the Lord, being fruitful and pleasing in every good work, increasing in the knowledge, strengthened with all His might according to his glorious power. Now one thing she did, forget about those things that were behind and is straining toward what is ahead.

God said to BB, now I have set before you an open door, a door of opportunity, a door opening to the 'Dawn of a new day' walk ye in it.

CHAPTER 11

DELAYED FORGIVENESS

Lord, how often shall my brother sin against me, and I forgive him? (Matthew18:21).

These words continued to haunt and assault BB's senses daily. She began to rehearse them in her mind. She felt as though she was bathing in a sea of synonyms such as: un-forgiveness, relentlessness, anger, bitterness, and hatred. She was a target for bitterness as she watched her in–laws betrayed her, friends disappointed her and even some of her family members forsaking her. BB was dying slowly, mentally, physically, emotionally and spiritually due to unresolved hurts, wounds, dependencies and addictive behavior of her spouse.

She did not know then like she knows now, that God was calling her to a whole new life of accountability to be healed and overcome those things which kept her and her children bound and blinded by the truth that was meant to set them free. But first BB have to ask God for His forgiveness for not believing and trusting in Him from the beginning. Also, to forgive those who have hurt and wrong her.

She discovered that the word forgiveness is to set a prisoner free and later learnt that prisoner was her. After falling into this predicament and bondage area, she ran to God and began to look into the mirror and pleaded with Him for help to show her how to gain victory in this area of life. She begged Him to forgive her hurts and help her to reconcile with all those who drove her to act and behave in an unsaved manner. BB asked him to let her experience the joy of letting go of her anger and hatred which was blocking her spiritual growth and hindering her spiritual blessings.

BB wanted God to help her to be patient; thoughtful and considerate. Even though people's ways and their motives, irritated, upset, provoked and disturbed her peace of mind by words and actions, she still wanted to remove from her heart all animosity she had towards them and not returned evil for evil, unkindness for unkindness, harsh words and sarcastic comments. To BB Un-forgiveness was like acid. It was doing more damage to the vessel in which it was stored then on the victims upon which it was poured.

BB continue to ask for forgiveness from all of her grumbling and complaining. All she wanted was God to teach her how to follow the example of Jesus who in his trials and tribulations said "Not my will but thine be done". In that same frame of mind, be able to face whatever life has in store for her. Another thing she wanted, was, God to give her grace to pattern her conduct after His Word.

BB shortcomings were due to her ignorance and hardness of heart which almost destroyed her spirit of pride. She did not want to waste the rest of her life consumed with tartness, animosity and irritation. She really needed help. Her emotional state made her cross and unpleasant, not only to herself but to her children at times. It was impossible for her to pray or to worship God while she was nurturing hateful thoughts of un-forgiveness. Matthew

6:15 clearly states: that her own forgiveness hinges on forgiving others. It does not say, do it when she felt like it. All it was saying, to her, stop being bitter, blaming people, forgive completely and release all of her anger to God because the entrance to her future is not big enough to drag her past through. Vengeance may look sweet but its effects, hurts its prey more than the perpetrator.

This had helped BB to create in her mind a special plot one which, she decided to bury all the faults of life. She wanted to be kind to one another, tenderhearted, forgiving one another, even as God in Christ has forgiven her. BB was also encouraged not to hate her brother in her heart and in no wise rebuke her neighbors and wish any sin upon them. She must not avenge, nor bear any grudge against them, but shall love her neighbors as she loves herself.

Her life experiences had taught her that she can depend on God as He continue to say to her that she must love her enemies, bless them who curse her and do good to those who hate her and pray for those who despitefully use and persecute her (Matthew 5:44). As tough as this seemed, God granted BB the desire to forgive others. Even though the process was slow and hard to carry through, she had decided to start her life afresh with the slate wiped clean of past mistakes thus feeling a heavy weight lifted from her shoulders. BB continued to pray for enough love in her heart and balance in her soul to forgive herself which was the greatest gift of all.

During this transformation in her life, like a clenched fist, she closed the window to her heart against all who hurt her. She has found out that as long as she harbored malice in her heart, she effectually hindered God's ability to work in her family's life and in her life. Again, God does not give her the right to revenge. This right belongs to Him and Him alone. Vengeance is His and He will recompense. Enmity had placed BB in a position reserved only for God she must never pay no one evil for evil. She must always have regard for good things in the sight of all men".

As God broke Satan's stranglehold on BB's life, He encouraged her to take up the shield of faith which will successfully extinguish all the flaming arrows of the evil one (Ephesians 6:16). Now her personal pain sets her mind on things above where genuine fulfillment can only be found. She must set your mind on things above, not on things on the earth. BB's life took a different twist. She chose a better way of living. When the threshing came over her, the grace of God shone round about her as pure gold. People who hurt her now, she refused to fight back because she has chosen God as her controller, her wrestler, her bodyguard to fight for her. The devil is a liar.

Through her relationship with God, she has learned that people hurt Jesus. It was a nasty circle. They whipped him, spat on him, then killed him all for nothing so who was she? In all of this, God never fought back. Instead, God forgave them all. What a spellbound lesson to be learned by all. Though there are times the wounds seemed too deep to heal and the chasm of misunderstanding seemed too wide to leap across, after knowing how Jesus did it, gave BB the incentive to pray fervently and consistently for God's guidance to close the wounds and narrow the gap between her with love, understanding and forgiveness. Life is too short.

BB started by asking God to forgive her for doubting His faithfulness and for questioning Him. She thanked Him for helping her to understand that all of her disappointments and sufferings are not a result of His neglect but rather His call to repentance. She asked God to continue to correct her when she fail Him. To use her disillusions as an occasion for prayer and for humble dependence on Him. Her lot in life would be nothing but misery and continual heartache but God is gracious and forgiving. He blessed her in spite of her sins. All she needed was Him to teach her through His word what He has promised to do in her life.

God did exactly what He had promised to do. He began to teach BB through His word and His Holy Spirit a new love, peace and power that enabled her to experience a new lifestyle. She felt like someone had plugged her into a vacuum and removed every bit of stench and guilt and replaced it with a new peace that was beyond her understanding". Then 2 Corinthians 5:17 explains it all, it affirmed that: "If anyone is in Christ, he is a new creature, old things will pass away, and behold all things will become new".

BB knew she had experienced what this verse of scripture had offered. One by one, God began to remove the old, corruptible habits from her life which held her capture for many, many long years. Now daily, she is feeding upon the Word of God for her daily intake of spiritual food and vitamins for strength and good health. On her menu God had placed this recipe of forgiveness on her table:

8	Oz. can of	Faith
8	Oz. bottle	Obedience
5	Cups of	Respect
2	Cups of	Gratitude
1	Bottle of	Inspiration
4	TSPS of	Victory
2	Cups of	Encouragement
1	Tin of	Nutrient
1	Dash of	Essence
3	TBSP of	Sharing
A	Dose of	Success

After carefully studying the menu, BB realize that in order to rise above her problems all she had to do was mix all of those ingredients together and season it to taste for an eternity of 'TRUE FORGIVENESS'.

CHAPTER 12

HEALING – NO MORE SCARS

In the middle of its street, and on either side of the river, was the tree of life, which bore twelve fruits, each tree yielding its fruit every month. The leaves of the tree were for the healing of the nation (Revelation 22:2)

But to you who fear my name the Sun of Righteousness shall rise with healing in His wings; and you shall go out and grow fat like stall-fed calves. (Malachi 4:2)

"Heal me O Lord, and I shall be healed. Save me, and I shall be saved, for thou art my praise. (Jeremiah 17:14).

Do you know how badly it hurts to wake up every morning, look into a mirror only to see the reflection of a bag of bones staring back at you; a corroded frame struggling with severe pains every day, and everywhere it goes the fire inside its columns continue to blaze? Do you realize how frightening and embarrassing it is to have to drag to work every day with drops of blood falling in the inside of you from the night's hammerings? That was BB. She felt like a failure.

Those were BB's scars. They ran very deep. Her wounds were agonizingly and slow in healing. Memories lingered, waiting to be singe with the branding iron of her own battery. Trust was broken and lines of communication were locked so tight. She was all wrapped up in her personal concerns and challenges that she allowed her hurts to take center stage in her life. BB was living in a bubble on another planet making it difficult to come out at the other end of the tunnel to see daylight. She became the mistress of her own destiny. It was so hard for her to enjoy life. She did not have the assurance about today, nor did she had the peace of yesterday and the self–confidence about tomorrow. There was always something going on in her life that she did not know how to deal with. She needed faith. She was faced with overbearing pains gripping her flesh from daylight to dark.

BB did not know how to handle this situation until she read where God said to Paul "My grace is sufficient for you and my strength is made perfect in weakness' (2 Corinthians 12:9). Then she learned that God will never lead her where He cannot keep her. It was at that time she was not only seeing God's face, but also His glory hidden away in the clef of the rock protected by His hand. BB began to learn how to lean and depend on Jesus. Through this learning experience, she began to find strength to sustain her in all the difficulties of her life. Her constant weeping before the Lord made her aware that there were angels nearby listening, calling, protecting and encouraging her.

God was delivering BB out of the paws of the gigantic bear. It made her to understand that in times of trials and tribulations, she is going to face giants. Some huge, some small and some maybe very fierce. But with God on her side, she would not have to face them alone nor does she have to be fearful.

After deep meditation, BB began to drop her fears into the ocean and watched them vanish one by one from sight. The things that were stolen from her and caused her to lose her identity, began restoring one day at a time. Through it all, she kept alive an embryo of hope in her heart because she knew for sure that her Redeemer lives. Hope made her to see the possibilities of a new life beyond her struggles. Hope made her see that Satan attacks all who dare to do the will of God. His tactics are legion. He used his prejudice and his stereotyping ways to steal her freedom and equality. He used labels such as shame, disgrace and limited capacity to strip away her dignity, self – worth, credibility and salvation. He tried to break her like he tried God's servant Job, His son Jesus, Moses, Daniel, Joshua and other great and powerful men in the Bible.

Now, when BB is suffering, she no longer had to ask why, because, God made her to know that it is only for a season and that troubles don't last always. He also made her to know, that suffering has meaning and when all around her the storms chum, the sea rages fast and furious, the fire burns and even in her hours of tears and bitterness that He has a solution for her where His strength flows like a river of healing waters. A place where she will be able to immerse herself and bask in its current and become renewed.

He had a place where, BB would be free from whatever binds, confines, entangles, oppresses or depresses her. A place where the spirit of heaviness can be lifted and her joy restored so that she can praise and glorify Him. Now, today, the presence of God's Holy Spirit has secured BB's freedom from living in 'Hell on earth' but she can finally say the wherever the Spirit of God is, there is liberty. Therefore, BB is now standing fast in liberty wherewith Christ hath made her free and not entangled again with the yoke of bondage.

God knew that all BB ever craved for was His living water to flow deeply, widely and expansively throughout that being of hers. He knew all she ever yearned for was His river of healing waters to fill her to overflow, to guide her until she becomes a remote temple from which a branch from His river can flow.

This healing experience taught BB how to value her thorns. It showed her how to climb the ladder to God through the path of her pain. Now, she has the victory of learning not to repeat the same mistakes. She had won over the devil and his imps. She had seen her beacon of light in this dark world of sin. God was promising her that through her tears, she would see her rainbow. She knew that this was all for Christ's good, she must be content in her weaknesses, insults, hardships, persecutions and calamities. For when she is weak, then will she be strong. Thank God for her life experiences and for His faithfulness to His promises for her.

Another truth that was revealed to her during her healing process, was that God allowed her to go through these trials to develop her gifts. Gifts that would never have been discovered but would have remained hidden if it was not for her ordeal. He allowed the difficulties not to separate her from Him but to bring her closer to Him. BB can now say unto God 'Do not simply condemn me; but tell me the changes you are bringing against me' (Job10:2).

Patiently and with great endurance, BB started exercising her faith in God's deliverance. She began to follow His anointed leadership toward her promised land remembering that this time, when she passed through the waters she will not sink or drown, though the waters be deep and swift. When she passed through the river it will not overflow her. (Isaiah 43:2). If and when attacking fires of stress, surround her and the smoke of circumstances burn her eyes, she still will not be scorched. Even now, when she is walking through the valley of the shadow of death, she is fearing no evil because God will be with her and will refine her like a precious metal. All was required of her was to listen, obey and respond when God speaks. Also, to allow Him to walk her through step by step her recovering process.

Her suffering was not in vain. God did not allow her to go through all of this just so she can use them in the future, He wanted her to know that, no matter what she had been through, he expects her to use her troubled – experiences so that others would benefit from them.

God has now restored BB's identity. She opened the door to her heart and let God's light shine through, no other light but Jesus Christ. A light she would follow every day for the rest of her life, aiming with all her strength to reach the end of her era growing richly and choosing excellence. This is her testimony.

Today, BB thank God for the love that He gave her. He instilled in her, that, love is not always meek and mild, nor is it always gentle and kind. He taught her that sometimes love is firm and tough but it is no less love. There she was becoming a beggar of love and healing, pleading and crying out for them both, knowing that all the love she was looking for was right within her spiritual being and in abundance. She was suffering because she was looking for love in all the wrong places.

Leaving her struggles and her anger, was like wriggling out of a cruel, burning skin. At last, she was seeing the beauty of the world through her healing. She is now transformed and made beautifully whole. BB insignificance became her significant. Her weakness became her strength. Her sorrow became her joy. It was through the Word of God the Holy Spirit spoke to her personally that she must remain still and know that He is God. Therefore, she is taking time to be silent and listen to God's voice. She is standing firm in the darkness knowing there is something solid there and that is healing enough for everyone.

From all of this, BB's wounds which had been so crude were healed without a scar. She had been too long feeling sorry for herself. This transformation took place during her lonely hours with God. It gave her new strength for each day. When things go wrong in her life because they will continue to, all she has do is pray through songs of praise and thanksgiving. During this period in her life these two favorites songs were her soother 'Turn your eyes upon Jesus' and 'Lord You are beautiful'. These really worked for BB.

Yesterdays and yesteryears disappointments cannot and will not stop BB now from serving her God. It is through Him she got her breakthrough and also a break free from the cocoon of inferiority and sycophancy. Instead of sitting down, with a deep breath, she arose from her struggles and began to stand way into the midnight with her head held high listening to a calm sweet voice saying "Behold! I stand at the door and knock. If any man hears my voice and open the door, I will come in to him and sup with him and he with me (Revelation 3:20). The voice continued BB know you are not strong, but you have tried to be obedient on numerous occasions and have not denied my name, therefore, again, I have placed before you an 'Open door of health and healing in which no man can shut'. "I am the doorkeeper and the key to your door". BB knew it was the voice of the Lord.

She began to asked, 'Lord why was it your feet delayed?' But thanks anyway for clothing her all over with your spiritual armor when she hit the rough bumps in the road. Thank You for shielding and healing her when she was battered, bruised, injured and badly broken. Thank You for clothing her with the shoes of the gospel of peace, when things could have grown much worse, had she, not listened to Your cautioning voice and Your invitation which is free to all. Lord, thank You, she could not have done it alone. You have given her the key to solving all of her problems. Your decisions were right your lessons were true.

To BB, it felt like it took forty years to find her way out. The testing, trials, darkness, storms, frightening shadows and the fears for the future are now erased from her life leaving 'NO MORE SCARS'. The healing process was successful. The sun is now shining through her back door. How can she ever give up with all the good You have done and are doing for her over and over. You came to her when she needed You the most. You turned her turmoil into triumph and gave her a new life. She thanked and praise God for replacing the dark ashes of her past with beautiful new joy in You. You anointed her with oil of happiness and gladness. You took away her mourning. You placed a garment of praise on her shoulders in place of the spirit of despair. You gave her a zest for living.

Thank You God for using BB's trials to teach her wisdom, empathy and compassion. Your warm constant presence has filled the void within her as she nested in the comforting arms of the Holy Spirit. Day and night she heeds Your Word and treasured Your peace within her heart and mind. A peace that soothes like a sunrise and flows through her like a gentle stream. A peace that floods and washes over the trials and stress with powerful, cleansing waves of righteousness. You stood nearby and watched while her impurities slowly burned away. Thank You for how She has learned to retrieve the lively warm fires and to leave the sad, cold ashes behind. It is because of You, she is now able to sit around with family members and acquaintances and joked about her past experiences. It is here she can certainly say with great confidence that; Forgiveness lingers like a healing balm lifting a huge weight from her shoulders.

BB's healing also reminded her, how Jesus carried her cross from darkness into light. This challenged her to trimmed away some fluff and release some unnecessary baggage at the foot of the cross. The cross became her altar because that is what the altar is for. She did not have to carry those burdens anymore. It was there her dead flesh was brought back to life. All her pain and anguish gave way to acceptance, healing and understanding. Her broken wings were made whole and BB soared into the haven of safety. In the midst of her challenges, the scab dropped from her eyes. With arms out stretched, she asked God to give her a clean heart and renew a right spirit within her (Psalms 51:10) and blow her to new levels of awareness.

Now BB can say of the Lord, He is her refuge and her fortress, her God in Him she trusts. His presence comforted her and gave her courage to keep going no matter what her circumstances were. With God as her guide, she found a safe passage. When waters seem to rage out of control, she found assurance in Matthew11:28 which reads, "Come unto me all ye who labored and are heavy laden and I will give you rest".

BB know now that God will never abandon her and He will always bring healing to her lonely heart. He had provided a safety net for her even in her hostile environment and from a home that had treated her like an outcast. Like Paul, she was crucified with Christ. There she was sitting in the midst of her darkness not knowing that a flame of light with a determine flicker was guiding her through the hopelessness and despair to a place of peace. She was not seeing the flashing neon billboard dangling in the air up ahead declaring 'There is healing scar-free'. She was then understanding the well – known words of the song, God works in mysterious ways his wonders to perform. God was truly working behind closed doors for her.

God, through His Holy Spirit was leading her to a room in the lighthouse with its beacon of light shining bright directing the ships through the misty air and fog, to the safety of her harbor with the assurance that the light, of hope will be swapped with the joy that she had never experienced and will reside in her heart forever. Thank God for such a revelation.

To summarize it all, BB was so thankful that she sought God's face for her healing because there is healing in that name. She now realizes that no problem is too big for God. If it gets bigger, if it increases, the grace of God will also increase. He is big enough to handle whatever she faces because what is impossible with men, is possible with God (Luke 18:27). His grace will always be available and sufficient for all. She once was dead and dry, now she is brought back to life. The pain and anguish gave way to acceptance and understanding. BB once broken wings are whole again and now ready to take flight for it is in God she put her trust.

Finally, BB confess that God is good! He has been and still is faithful to her. He has never failed her and will never fail her in the future. Even when bad things try to come up against her, God will be right there to save and deliver her. He has brought her out of it all with no permanent harm. It is a miracle she survived everything that happened to her in the past. Now from this moment on, she chooses to turn her memories around and reflect on how God has been good to her through all of life's events. BB sought the Lord and He heard her and delivered her from all her fears. She waited on Him. He became her rock, her salvation and her defense. God numbered her wanderings and put her tears in a bottle and left them there. Her flesh and her heart failed but God was the strength of her heart and became her portion forever.

CHAPTER 13

GROWING FROM STRENGTH TO STRENGTH – PRAYER LIFE

Philippians 4:6–8 declare: "Be anxious for nothing, but in everything by prayer and supplication with thanksgiving, let your requests be made known to God and the peace of God, which surpasses all understanding will guard your hearts and minds through Christ Jesus. Finally, brethren whatsoever things are noble, just, pure, lovely and are of good report, if there be any virtue and if there is anything praiseworthy meditate on these things".

"Come unto me all you who labor and are heavy laden, and I will give you rest. Take my yoke upon you and learn from me, for I am gentle and lowly in heart, and you find rest for your souls. For my yoke is easy and my burden is light". (Matthew 11:28-29 KJV)

BB admitted here that she has been delinquent in her prayer life. She has been trying to pull her entire load by herself mostly without prayer. She has given it every ounce of her strength until she simply could not handle it any longer. It became evident that she could not change herself without the help of God. Restraint, moderation, temperance, discipline, self – control and patience were parts of her life that were missing and needed to be developed. She had found that, in her own strength, she was no match for life's problems. Was it that she was afraid to pray or really did not know how? These were questions which kept on surfacing. This however, brought her to a dead – end in her life. It was by faith that she did not go insane or lose her mind. The stress, the strain and depression she was experiencing was getting so severe that she learned, the only answer was to immerse herself in the Word of God, stand on His promises and spent some quality and quiet time with the Lord in intense prayer.

Instantly, BB began to meditate and confess her sins to God. Being alone with Him, she gave Him all of her problems. As she began to converse with God in a way like never before, her mind became clearer and clearer to the truth. For God in His Word promised her a sound mind and that was exactly what she needed then. She was seeking for God to safeguard her emotions, invade and shelter her from the arrows the enemy was shooting at her in order to arouse a spirit of fear in her and to defend her mind from all the demonic assaults.

At that moment, BB admitted to God her weaknesses and brokenness. She humbly begged Him for strength to carry her through many, many days. She begged Him to donate to her a fresh supply of His Holy Spirit and his forgiveness for other things that had dominated and distracted her from being in His presence. She begged Him to give her the fortitude to say no to those things that kept pulling her away from praying as she should and not let her be like the Pharisees who when they prayed heaped up repeated phrases that were multiplying words. BB asked for forgiveness for the sin of ungodly rage and anger and for all those in her life who have hurt or wounded her and even for those who she have supposedly hurt and even judged, she asked forgiveness.

Even for the times when Lids had fallen into a low – level of entertaining phrases such as: "You have scratch my back and I will scratch your back". "Tick for tack is fair play." 'An eye for an eye and a tooth for a tooth" 'You kill my dog I will kill your cat'. Her heart leaped When God said vengeance belongs to You.

BB prayed consistently with a conviction in accordance with God's Word and his will. She began to develop a simple faith - believing prayer asking God for boldness and clarity of speech and confidence even if she only say, 'God, please help her, save her, bless her and hear her plea. For, she knew that God hears and answers prayers as long as her request was in accordance with His will. As she prayed, she began to developed a close personal and intimate relationship with God.

During those times alone with God, her life became more solid, sound, secure, stable and more powerful. Like a grain of mustard seed planted, BB began to watch her prayer life grow from "Strength to Strength". She then chose to make a declaration to walk away from all the horror that was taking place in her life. She decided to dump everything that was displeasing, distasteful and desecrating to the Holy Spirit that was dwelling within her in the sea of forgetfulness and walk away from every negative thought, word and deed that had tried to operate in her that was dishonoring to God.

BB's goal was to turn in a new direction. To walk a new walk and talk a new talk that showed respect and love for God. This awakened her to the reality that Satan did not have the power to keep her down and depressed. She was giving Satan too much credit. There were still times when she felt distraught and could not pray, the Holy Spirit was right there present to guide her through. Because of her consistent prayer life, the Holy Spirit now lives in her and the nature of Jesus Christ has also developed in her. She is feeling Him daily in her heart. What an overwhelming feeling to know that Christ now lives in her helping her to see herself as His dwelling place and to honor His presence.

Today, BB is so thankful that God had not abandoned her to self and emotions. Now she can happily say that she is washed in the fruit of joy and peace. This gave her the incentive to pursue the agape love a high - level love she longed acquired. A love of utmost importance in every area of her life. A love that has helped her soar to a higher realm manifested in her life. BB prayed for God to work mightily in her life making these attributes goodness, faithfulness, longsuffering and kindness an integral part of her daily living. She is so elated to report that her prayer life is now the key to her success.

As BB prayed, she became more and more Christ – like. She became less and less aware of self and more and more of Jesus. God had implanted in her, mercy, grace, compassion, righteousness and justice which no human could ever do. He had made her eyes, ears, hands, feet and mouth all His. He is now 'Yoked' with her in her family, ministry, job and in all her personal affairs. God has now become her 'Biggest Helper'. Because of His strategic role in her life, her attitude, her environment, her work and everything connected to her, her life has now become better, finer and more pleasurable.

BB's life assignment is surely not a burden now but truly a delight. It was through her prayers she had found the links that connected her with God in the abyss of danger, toil and snare; the problem fixer to every can – of – worms as they come along whether they appear in small or big packages. Now, she will never underestimate the power of prayer and the power of God's Word. It is full of good stuff she never knew existed during her abusive situation. God's Word continues to water her daily. She indulged God's supernatural peace to take up residence and serve as an umpire and a referee for her heart and mind and to energize her for the completion of her divine assignment. BB declared that she is now filled and charged with the Spirit of God where there will be no lack of strength. She had no more time left, to 'hit or miss' or even fall short of the plan God has for her life.

To all those who are weak in God's faith, BB says to you, now is the time to push pass flesh and other uninvited invaders that plague you. Attach yourself with a band of believers and prayer warriors to help strengthen your faith. Pray and let God's Word guide you. Permit God to rub His anointed hand upon your life and let the powerful sweet fragrance of the anointing be felt, sensed and seen in you by others who are near you. God did it for me and He will do the same for you. He is only a heartbeat away just waiting for your call. Why not let Him in? The best result for your breakthrough is 'Praying and Believing! For God's Word declares that: 'Greater is He that is in you than He that is in the world'. BB believed that she had entered into a harvest producing season, one that she will never leave. God became her source of nourishment. She is now God's special fruit garden, to be watered daily and treated with special care.

Friends, family and colleagues, prayers forced a passage through BB's iron clad bars and brazen gates and sat an angel at the door of her heart who touched and healed all her wounds. Her prayers now are all 'Thank you' prayers. All she feels is indescribable peace which surpassed all understanding which come from God her Father and her dearest friend. What a friend to have in Jesus? He just waiting on you to bring all your grief and sorrows to Him. He counted it a privilege to bring everything to Him in Prayer.

God came to her warning 'Don't stop praying' and she obeyed Him. Prayer has become an important part of her daily routine. She now has something to sing and shout about, to boast about and to crow about. I've got King Jesus and as long as I've got King Jesus I don't need anybody else. BB cannot stop thanking God for His hand of mercy, for victory obtained by His son Jesus through his resurrection from the dead and who invaded hell and broke the power of its demonic state just for me.

BB became destined that every time she entered her prayer chamber, she would ask God to clothed her with His whole armor. To girdle her with truth, the helmet of salvation, the breastplate of righteousness, the shield of faith, and even shoes so that her feet will be shod with the preparation of the gospel of peace, and the sword of the spirit as her weapon so that she will be able to stand against all the wiles of the devil. She knew she had to be prepared because, she could not wrestle against flesh and blood but against principalities, against powers, against the rulers of the darkness of this age, against spiritual host of wickedness in the heavenly places so that she will be able to withstand in the evil day.

Now when BB looks in the mirror, she likes what she sees. She sees someone who already has the victory. She possessed the authority to keep the devil under her feet where he belongs. BB is so glad she learned to trust in Jesus and took him at his Word. Her discovery was, God did not want to just give her strength all He wanted was, to be her strength. Alleluia. BB is now blessed. Blessed be the name of the Lord!

She could not survive without prayer. Try it. It works for every situation. Don't stay in a condition all tied and tangled up. Sing! Sing unto the Lord a new song every day. Show forth His salvation from day to day. Declare His glory among the heathen and His wonders among all people (Psalms 96:1–3). That is how God's humble servant David did it. He has been and still is an inspiration in BB's prayer life. She can see clearly now the rain is gone she can certainly smile. Whenever she cries now it is not tears of sorrow but tears of joy. Thank You Lord for Your blessing on her.

In closing BB says to her readers none of us are perfect and we all fall short of God's glory at times. When we are trying to change and trying to strive to be all that God wants us to be, we make Him proud. The Word of God indicates, that, we must confess our sins to one another. We are no different than any other human. Some people may say they have never done anything wrong, but we all have done wrong and had wrong things done to us in the past that we are not proud of, so, continue pressing forward. Do not look back. Let the past be the past. Leave those things behind. Run and reach for the prize of His High calling which is Christ Jesus. For in Him the road ahead is paved with good intentions and many blessings just for you.

CHAPTER 14

LIGHT AT THE END OF THE TUNNEL

But you are a chosen generation, a royal priesthood, a holy nation, His own special people, that you may proclaim the praises of Him who call you "Out of darkness into His marvelous light". (1 Peter 2:9).

Behold, I will do a new thing, now it shall spring forth, shall you know it? I will even make a road in the wilderness and rivers in the desert (Isaiah 43:19).

If you go the wrong way – to the right or to the left - you will hear a voice behind you saying, "This is the right way" (Isaiah 30:21).

During BB's trials and tribulations, it was so intense, that she felt as if she was heading somewhere but was not enjoying the ride. Her eyes grew very dim, it felt like the tunnel in the vein leading to her brain and the rest of her body was so dark, hot and humid and the pathway so dusty and rocky with BB's feet, all battered and bruised. Her clothes all tattered and torn. Her inside so arid and parched for lack of drinking water and the Living water. She found herself stumbling, staggering and grapping for a way out.

As she limped along, it felt as if creepy crawlers were nipping her flesh as she tried to hold on for dear life and reached out for help.

Feeling faint, dog tired, and distressed she crumbled and knelt in the dust of the earth. A weird coldness came over her. A feeling she could not described. As she knelt there shaking like a leaf in a hurricane, her soul cried out silently, 'Lord, lead me, guide me, along the way, let your Word be a lamp to my feet and a light to my path (Psalm119:105). Release me out of that underground passage, that cave, tube, burrow and tunnel. Illuminate, ignite and inflame my pathway. Open my eyes that I may see'.

There BB remained stunned for a while like a wounded bird caught in a prison of destitution, abandonment and confined in an iron – clad cell, trembling, desperately waiting for this nightmare to end. Waiting for the walls of this tunnel to open. Walls that she could not penetrate for the freedom of her soul. Within moments of her grief, Solomon came to mind in Proverbs 3:5-6) "Trust in the Lord with all thine heart and lean not unto your own understanding. In all thine ways acknowledge Him and He will direct thy paths.

In realization, Solomon was saying to BB that in order to find her way out of that tunnel she must trust the Lord wholeheartedly and always be on the alert to His direction in every way. The Psalmist David also emphasized that, she must allow the Lord to order her steps in His Word and not let any circumstances of the world have dominion over her.

Then God took BB on a trip to Bible days when great men were surrounded by darkness and how they overcame it. He said take a look at Joseph, how he went from the 'Pit to the Palace'. Moses, how he survived his wilderness experiences forty days and nights in spite of the continuous murmurs and complaints of the Israelites. The prophet Daniel, Shadrack, Meshach and Abednego, because of their faithfulness and obedience to the one and only true God were delivered from the terrible scorching flame of fire that were seven times hotter than usual. Daniel who also was delivered from, a den of ferocious lions.

When He took her to Elijah's experience on Mount Carmel, it was there when something struck her. BB's mind began to think silently, what about His Son Jesus Christ? It was Him who was tortured and beaten viciously, barbarously and heartlessly for her sake, then, as if that was not enough, plaited a crown out of sharp thorns we called prickles and placed it upon his head, hung Him and crucified Him. He could have saved himself but no He went through it all for her sake – your sake because he loves us unconditionally. What a man? He is one to admire and love with all our heart, mind and soul forever. BB agreed with the songwriter when he sang "Above All" how Jesus laid behind a stone, rejected and all alone. Like a rose he was trampled on the ground but he thought of me and took the fall.

It was here BB paused and cried out and asked the Lord to show himself to her. Teach her how to pray like how He taught his disciples because she has no words left. She could only sit and think. Immediately, God interrupted her thoughts and said, "It's not only words I can hear but also silent prayers and groans I do not refuse for I too understand unspoken requests. At the same time, He bent down a little closer and continued, 'My child, I am here to deliver you. I will take the load off you just lean heavily on me and your road will become smoother for it must get rough before it is smooth. You must get out of the habit of asking for a silver lining in your storm clouds. Get out of the habit of grumbling and complaining like the ungrateful Israelites.

Stop yielding to discouragement. I have never failed anyone who honestly and sincerely call on my name. Have patience and believe not just with a part of your heart but with your whole heart. No matter how severely stressed you may be, never slow down or you will choose to eat the dust of bitter defeat. For it is in the past now, that you were full of darkness, but now you will be full of light in Me. So, live like a child who belong to the light. Light brings every kind of goodness, right living and truth. Try to learn what pleases me. Have nothing to do with the things done in darkness, which are not worth anything. But show that they are wrong (Ephesians 13-14), So, get up! And I will guide you in the right path to the open door of your tunnel" says the Lord. Suddenly, BB came to the reality that dark days do not last forever. That was her rainy season of suffering giving way to a brighter tomorrow.

Slowly, BB rose to her feet she recognized that God was preparing her for new beginnings. She stretched her hands toward heaven and cried aloud "Thank You God for this revelation. He then had given her the boldness and enthusiasm to let go of the old and accept the new. She then heeded God's word and obeyed His instructions. Just as her pathway was lined with thick blackness, so to, was each painful experience lined with a miracle of lessons to be learnt. BB knew she could not guide herself through that dark and wet tunnel alone so she decided to look into the very heart of the darkness and refused to yield to its paralyzing influence.

This time when BB began walking through the tunnel, the way got easier, the burdens got lighter one step at a time. Gradually, the veins of her eyes became more visible from the sunbeam lining the tunnel of her eyes. The presence of the light enlightened her. Unseen incandescence began to roll back the gloom as she neared the end of her journey. Shadows dispel, spirits were broken. Her eyes began to see a glimpse of the outside world. Her soul began to flood with an unknown glow. For the first time in all of this, BB was not seeing through her eyes naturally but Spiritually. The Lord became her lamp and enlightened her darkness. She felt her life turning around for good.

God wanted BB to come up into the light and see the sunshine for herself and to let her know that after the rain the sun does shine. Gladly she accepted the invitation to rise. BB began to see the sun glistening on the sides of her tunnel. The blue firmament began to peek through a hole somewhere. BB began to hear little voices in her head urging her on like chorus of little angels singing don't give up you have made it this far a little further would not hurt. Plodding along, she smelled fresh clean air. Her eyes became opened. There was she standing in awe with a Halo of light encircling her head surely and truly it was "the Light of the World' who was guiding her. Now she knows that no dark places could ever extinguish her light.

On reaching the end, BB shouted praises of thanksgiving to God. Se echoed, surely Jesus you are the Light of the World. When she stumbled through the darkness, you were by her side with your voice whispering, 'You can make it". When the walls of sorrow seemed insurmountable you were right there saying "Don't give up push on", When she was sinking in despair your hand reached out and grabbed her. God the water that filled her when she was all dried up of hope and faith. It is a great feeling to be cared for by the King of Kings and the Lord of Lords. Now she has given up all her worries and concerns to Him and is now enjoying the promise of His protection, stability and fullness of joy and also, her freedom from the dark dungeon.

There, God had exchanged the ashes from BB fire for serenity. The life lesson she had learned was that throughout the course of life, there will be times of tragedy, sorrow, fear, and confusion. There will be trials, troubles and tribulations. There will be times when it will appear to be no light and happiness but only a wisp of the wind floating away in the distance from her grasp making her feel lost and abandoned. All He required of her was, to follow the light given her by Him and He will show her the pattern in the quilt of her faith for her life. All BB had to do was draw near to Him and He will draw near to her and show her the plan He has for her life that will bring her His peace.

BB also thank God that he did not allowed her darkness to overpower her because His Word guarantees her that darkness does not have the ability to overcome the light. She is so thankful that she is God's child and that now she lives on the winning side of the fence. BB still gets knocked down occasionally but she never gets knocked out because God's favor is now on her life forever.

On completion, BB now says God has called her 'OUT OF DARKNESS INTO HIS MARVELOUS LIGHT'. He has given her the grace to live as His child of light and be a beacon of light to others who dwell in darkness so they too can glorify Him through His choices and actions and be drawn to Him who is definitely the light.

The Lord has single BB out for special blessings not shared by others. He taught her how to remember them and count them one by one. She discovered that she was walking down the wrong lane in the road, looking for answers. She was looking to the wrong sources for help such as parents and other family members and friends to lead her through her valley of denseness. BB was expecting them to give her that which only God could have given her such as, peace of mind, security, contentment, confidence in the outcome of life and a sense of joy. Now it is only in God that she lives, moves and have her being. Thank You! It is because of her faithfulness and obedience she is now receiving her harvest. It is through God's grace BB is able to attack her giants. She has finally crossed over the Jordan river into the land where she has never seen or passed before. She also realized that her trials were only an opportunity for her victory. God's love will not let her go so she rest her weary head upon His shoulders and yield her flickering torch to Him as His light followed her all the way to a brighter fairer day. This is also a part of BB's testimony of her wilderness experience of 'OUT OF DARKNESS INTO MARVELLOUS LIGHT'. Thanks again Lord for Your Blessings on me.

CHAPTER 15

REJOICE WITH ME –
FREE AT LAST

BB finally came out of her bondage, sorrow, and night and into God's freedom gladness, and light. She finally came out of her sickness into good health, out of her wants and into God's wealth, out of her sin and into herself, out of her shameful failure and loss, out of earth's sorrows and out of distress direct into God's jubilant Psalms. She heard the promises of God's everlasting love and kindness speaking to her and she quickly responded Jesus I come to Thee.

What comfort this brought BB in every area of her life. She had found herself in many difficult situations like the Psalmist David, panting, like a deer for water to fulfill the deep longing thirst for God to ease her pain. She was just like an onion with layers and layers of misfortunes. An ugly onion that is, whose stench was so strong. But thank God for Jesus. Unbeknown to her, he bought her and love her all the time despite the odor. He did this without her having a clue of what he was going to do or what He was planning for her.

In the meantime, God was secretly pulling each layer off of BB one day at a time in order to make her more like Jesus, His son. The first layer, He lifted her slowly from 'Behind prison walls' from "A Disturbed Childhood' where harsh treatment occurred. Gradually, He began to peal layer after layer. Layers of Blind Contravention', her See–saw years, and 'Deserted and Alone'. She paused here, to thank the Lord for what He had done for her. This gave her the opportunity to change her attitude and focus her attention on the present moment. It gave BB the incentive, not to wait until she sees the end results or to receive rewards, she is thanking him right now for this disclosure.

As God continued to peel more layers of hurt from her marriage, the pain and suffering BB felt for her children, it began to hurt all the more. As He got closer and closer to the core, perplexed at what He might find there, she had no choice but to lay it all at Jesus feet. However, the process did not end there. God, noticing the unbearable pain, BB thinks He wept. The layers to brought Him much pain. The hurt and the suffering that she thought were about to disappear were all hidden and buried under these layers disguised in a salve so firmed. As He tore at the remaining layers, 'All that glitters are not gold', unveiling the mask she was hiding behind while she worked and her financial difficulties, BB again began to think that God's tears became uncontrollable equal to her own.

Both BB's Heavenly Father and her, were nearing the center of it all. This is where He ceased for a while and gave her a balm of comfort and security to sustain her. Some of her layers tore and pulled at her heart, whilst others grieved her to her innermost soul which made her screamed out in pain 'No more layers Lord' as He continue peeling and tearing. When will it end what should she do? She groaned. If He continues she would be nothing but a scraggly, scrawny, raw bone.

Instantly, she heard Him say, 'Just trust me as I finish my job. Upon completion, all was left of her was a shrunken tiny dried up red stem. The process was so powerful that it penetrated deep within her giving her a wake – up call. It helped her to understand, God's plan and purpose for her life. During this time, the lord embraced BB in His loving arms and said "Now and only now, you are free. You can be the creation that will minister before me, clothed with righteousness and truth from above". God had lifted a ton off her shoulders. He was her deliverer. Had it not been for the Lord, she would have been eternally lost. She owes a debt of gratitude to You Papa dear, for a price so high she really cannot pay.

BB thanked Him for loosening her chains and setting her 'Free' and for not giving up on her when others did by holding her hostage in their mind. She was bought with a price. The love and care God gave, are the priceless things that made her what she is today. After stripping her of all the layers, God has opened Lids eyes to the things that were blinding her. That is why she is still standing.

Now, BB do not need any one's sympathy at all. God has stood by her in the good and in the bad times. He helped her to succeed. He reminded her of his promises that he will take care of her. He told her to seek Him first and do His perfect will. Back then, it was because of her disobedience, she fell down, so, she began to seek Him intimately until she finally heard him say, 'you wanted me and you sought me out until I, God, finally heard your voice and surrendered to your call.

Today, BB is so happy that God pursued her personally and intimately with such passion and with such a mighty love. He refused to give up on her. Because of this, she got up from her fall. This gave her the will to live. She remembered the futility she felt as she tried to change herself but could not do it. But, when God stepped into her life, everything changed. Again, she paused to shout thanks and praises to God for loving her unconditionally.

Now BB has waved, goodbye to the rotten layers of sin and hello to love, joy, peace, gentleness, forgiveness, happiness, goodness, meekness, faith, hope and temperance all wrapped up in her newborn body. She changed her focus on championing a new course by doing away with the old and putting on the new. Lids is now an ambassador of positive thinking and a spectator to the negative generation. She took all the unhappy memories such as her anger, hate and resentment out of her body and placed them in a heavy steel basket, sinking it into the depth of the sea of forgetfulness making her free. The hold Satan had on her is miraculously smashed into fine pieces impossible to mend together again.

BB's life is now in full bloom. No matter the weather, she is growing sturdier and stronger spiritually daily. She is reaching upward for the prize in the sky and do so joyfully with the assurance that she is grounded in the life cycle of spiritual development. Now, when she looked back over her life and think things over, she can truly say that she has been blessed, she got a testimony. So, rejoice with her for, her life is now being snatched out of the jaws and paws of lions and tigers, snakes and scorpions, abusers and accusers. You see, there is nothing too hard for God. He is a great and miraculous God. No man can work like Him for there is none like him. He is the God who delights in making the impossible possible.

Everywhere BB goes now she represents Jesus Christ to her family, her place of employment, her neighborhood, her friends, her church and her home. She may not be a perfect witness, but, know for sure that she is a willing one. The Holy Spirit is her Helper, her Teacher and her Guide. Everything Jesus did for His chosen ones, the Holy Spirit is now doing for her.

The Holy Spirit is also leading and showing BB all her Heavenly Father wants her to be and do. She is feeling 'Royalty' and is fully covered with the blood of Jesus. Now she can call upon heaven to assist her at any given time because all of the angelic powers and all the vast resources are stored up for her in the treasury of heaven. They are now at her disposal and available for her use when she is representing Him in her country and the rest of the world. She is unshackled and free from the tyranny and cruelty of abuse. Thank God BB is free at last.

BB is completely different from the person she used to be. Jesus saw her confused hurting heart while she was facing her valley of decisions. Amidst the hurt and unanswered questions, God was always there with a listening ear and compassionate eyes watching her. He heard Lids cries and protests. When the heat was turned up, His love rose higher and higher. He saw and heard the injustice done to her. His mercies never dried up. His branches were always reaching far enough to cover her.

God was always there for her even in those moments of her greatest frustration. Because of this, He never allow her to go down in defeat. Whenever she looks into the mirror now, BB sees someone completely different. A brand new her on the move for Jesus. She sees someone who is ready to face any battle with the assurance that victory, joy and deliverance today is her own.

BB has no reason to be ashamed of who she is now. As she looks forward, she can see the tracks of obedience and faithfulness carrying her and walking beside her. She is now putting the devil on the run and beating him at his own game. She is making room for fresh biblical ideas, positive thoughts and honest opinions from other Christians soldiers. With this song in jubilation she crooned, "It is finish the battle is over, it is finish there will be no more war". God had fought all her battles for her. It was the end of the conflict and victory was her own for the claiming. Thank God Praise His name she is free. BB decree and declare the words of the Prophet Isaiah during his stormy periods: She passed through the waters and they did not overflow her. She walked through the fire and did not get burn neither did the flame kindle upon me. (Isaiah 43: 2).

A song of freedom, a song of praise, a song of victory. Now from her rooftop BB can finally echoed the words of Dr. Martin Luther King jnr.:

'Free at last, Free at last
Thank God I am free at last'.
Thank God I am 'FREE AT LAST'.

'Rejoice with her'.

CHAPTER 16

ADVICE – STOP! LISTEN! LEARN!

"Not by might nor by power, but by My spirit, says the Lord of host." (Zechariah 4: 6)

It was not by BB's might nor was it by her power, but by God's spirit that worked in her, she was able to break loose the chains of darkness. It was because of her will to stand on the promises of God's Word she won in the end. It is summed up well in the message of Proverbs 31 when it reads, May the work BB have done speak for her. Now she can turn this same phrase around and say, 'May the life she lived speak for her'.

BB's failures came because of her inexperienced childhood and lack of knowledge but as you can see, God woke her up and saved her life from death. He wanted her to have life and to have it in abundance. As she aforementioned, God wanted her to live and not die.

During the process, the time came when she stopped, listened, and learned with the help of St. Paul in 2 Corinthians 4:8–9 when he wrote, we are hard pressed on every side, yet not crushed; we are perplexed, but not in despair; persecuted, but not forsaken; struck down, but not destroyed.

She had experienced all of these conditions. She was crushed, persecuted, forsaken, perplexed, and even hard pressed on every side, struck down and almost destroyed, but, every day she turned to God in fervent prayer, seeking and asking Him to give her strength for the day and bright hope for tomorrow.

There were days when she was running scared for her life then she remembered that God had not forsaken her but was waiting for her to first 'Acknowledge' His presence. Secondly, to 'Stop', sit still and 'Know' that He is God. Thirdly, to 'Recognize' His presence because He is God of many chances. He is God who is always faithful to His Word and who does not lie. He said in His Word He will never leave us nor forsake us and she believed in Him and obeyed His Word. With God working in her, she could not help but be victorious.

Readers, when your battles continue to rage, you must believe that you are not fighting them alone. Sometimes they would be too big and seemed beyond repair, but always remember that God is always there speaking to you. When it seems like the vast ocean is about to overflow its shores please hold on. His invisible hands are your dam to stop a tsunami from engulfing you. Whenever you feel confused and wondering why every area of your life is under attack, hold on and give God the praise and glory with certainty that help is on its way. He will send out angels to make roads in the hills; put a hedge around you and even though it might seem mighty hot in the midst of it all and like thorns piercing your flesh, pay good attention to 2 Corinthians 12:9 when It says: 'My grace is sufficient for you, for My strength is made perfect in weakness.'

In not so many words God is telling you that His grace will be with you in your fiery furnace. It will help you to part the waters of your Jordan River, it will shut the mouths of the lions, fight your battles and bring down the walls of your Jericho. His grace will unloose the chains from off your feet and break the locks from the doors of your jail cells. Isn't this awesome to know? What a mighty God we serve. The one and only true God whose love is unending. After hearing and seeing all of this, BB asked God for a loving, forgiving and reconciling heart from the bitterness which crept its way secretly into her heart when she thought on the path her life took.

When she thought on the many times she went the extra mile for Jas and in – laws and the hurtful and painful experiences she encountered with them, causing her soul to be reflected from peace, and made her strength perished. Many times she was prone to give up and throw in the towel, but thank God for Jesus.

BB's marriage did not fail because she was too busy or being negligent, it failed because of Jas's substance abuse, lack of communication and his relationship not being God-centered.

But she is so grateful to God for granting her the opportunity to talk it out with Him in her quiet chambers. It was because of Him she is able to put the past totally in the past.

The ills of the world no longer direct her thoughts and emotions. Her past can never, ever get her down. God sees and knows everything. He is always right on time. He stepped right in and rescued her. Everywhere BB goes, people would ask, "Why are you so happy after all you went through?" her response is always the same, it is all God. He gave her His secret weapon and she is now elated to share it with others. BB has learned that there was very little she could have done by herself in her sufferings that would change the situations, she had to 'Stop!' 'Listen!' and 'Learn!' how to lean and depend on Jesus and accept him as her friend. She had to 'Stop', 'Listen', 'Learn' how to trust and rely on God through His Word and through consistent prayers. In that way, God had never let her down. That was her secret for a free and happy life.

To all the abusive and hurting women in the universe who are reading this book and have gone or going down this same path, BB says to you that is not the end. 'STOP' For a moment and read the Word of God which have helped her through her trying times and she knows it can help you to. Take a moment and 'Listen!' and 'Learn' what each scripture verse is saying to you. By doing this you will become a brand new person in God and yourself. You will see a change come over you from God's unique promises.

The first thing you have to do is stop and think. For example:

1. "Stop"!
   i   Sometimes you may feel like no one loves you but God does. John 3:16.
   ii There will be times you will say, Lord, I am too tired but God says He will give you rest. Matthew 11:28-30
   iii God also says, 'the pain that you have been feeling can't compare to the joy that's coming. Romans 8:18
   iv Cast your burdens on the Lord and he will sustain you. (Psalms 55:22- 2)
   v   Ask God to show you His paths and teach you truth. For He is the God of your salvation. A God you need all your days. (Psalms 25:4 – 5)

Here is a word of advice. Stop trying to fix, control and make things happen yourself. Turn it over to God. He has the perfect blue print for your life. Step back and examine your life and discover how to take your painful past and use it for God's glory and for your good.

2. "Listen!"
   i Trust God from the bottom of your heart: don't try to figure out everything on your own. Listen to God's voice in everything you do, everywhere you go, he is the one who will keep you on track. Don't assume that you know it all, run to God! run from evil. Proverbs 3:5 NIV

   ii Listen to advice and accept discipline, and at the end you will be counted among the wise. Proverbs 19:20 NIV

   iii Hearing and Doing the Word Know this, my beloved brothers: let every person be quick to hear, slow to speak, slow to anger; James 1:19 (ESV)

   iv The Lord will fight for you, and you have only to be silent." Exodus 14:14 English Standard Version (ESV)

   v And he said to them, "Pay attention to what you hear: with the measure you use, it will be measured to you, and still more will be added to you. Mark 4:24 ESV /

3. "Learn!"
   i Brothers, I do not consider that I have made it my own. But one thing I do: forgetting what lies behind and straining forward to what lies ahead. Philippians 3:13 ESV.

   ii Cast your burden on the Lord, and he will sustain you; he will never permit the righteous to be moved. Psalm 55:22

   iii Count it all joy, my brothers, when you meet trials of various kinds, for you know that the testing of your faith produces steadfastness. And let steadfastness have its full effect, that you may be perfect and complete, lacking in nothing. James 1:2-4 ESV

iv The Lord upholds all who are falling and raises up all who are bowed down. Ps.145:14

v Surely there is a future, and your hope will not be cut off. Proverbs 23:18

Finally, always walk in the truth. Put the storms of troubles and trials on God's altar every day and leave them there. No matter what happens in life, or what state or condition you find yourself in, keep on praying. God will stop, listen and work it out. He will create something new in and through you. Partners, listen when He speaks. Let your conversation with God bring healing to your past. Even though you maybe a product of the past, you are not a prisoner of it.

Do not let any disappointment stop you from praying. If you keep on climbing and talking to God, He will turn your sorrow and your hopeless situations into joy. In your prayers, ask God to show you what to do to deal with your sadness. Submit the yoke of your weight to Him that His will be done and not your will. It does not matter how deep your hurt or abuse is, God is able to vindicate it.

Follow your tears and you will find God. You will find the answer to how you should live. As for BB, she found a reason to live. She declares and decree that she shall live and not die to do the work of the Lord and to encourage others with her testimony of how God brought her out of her deep dark dungeon. She stopped and looked deep to find meaning and discovered that she has so much to give and share.

BB knows it is not easy for someone to talk about their pain. She knows how frightening it is to trust someone. She had to go to God in her quiet little room and cried out to Him. She remembered that God is only a prayer away. He is always there patiently waiting and watching to hear from you to let you know that troubles do not last always. They too will pass and shall not stay.

Learn from the mistakes in your life, in future look for warning signs, indicating 'danger ahead' this will stop you from going the wrong way. Let God be your support in all you do and choose. To be able to do this, you have to forgive and forget those who wronged you and who you have wronged.

1 Peter 2:9 (NIV) You are a chosen people, a royal priesthood, a holy nation, God's special possession, that you may declare the praises of him who called you out of darkness into his wonderful light.

Strive daily to know who you are and whose you are for your body is the temple of the Lord where the spirit of God dwells. It is your pavilion. It keeps you warm and dry but words of trouble can find its way in through cracks and seams of doors and windows of your pavilion and blow you down. People will also rip you apart and hurt you. The inescapable wetness of rainy days can make your feet damp and tired but you need to learn that there is a new and wonderful mansion prepared for you, where no wind can blow it away and where no one can rip the windows and doors apart.

Some days you will look through the window of your heart and see the sky tar-black with large clouds moving towards you and there is nothing you can do; then you hear tapping on the window it became a pitter-patter like heavy raindrops. In a daze you just sit there imagining people running for cover outside and umbrellas opened as the clouds spat out their beads of water against the door and window of your heart that is locked up with the troubles of the world. As the rainfall becomes heavier, you could hear the murmuring of the rain through the window sounding like a swarm of buzzing angry bees all around you.

To all the hurting women out there, this is a time when God is speaking to you in a still small voice. Let the raindrops out of your heart in a sweet spirit to God who is waiting to shower you with the blessings He has in store for you. Lift up your soul on wings of joy. He is right there ready to guide you from the chaos and shadows, out into the light of peace. Relax, it is all taken care of.

God does not want you to feel uncomfortable living in darkness and never seeing the sun, nor be contented suffering in a dungeon, walking up and down in that lowly conditions and lingering in its lowlands, afraid to climb the mountain because of its steepness and ruggedness. If you decide to stay in the mist of the valley you will never learn the mystery of the hills.

BB in her conclusion, is advising you, never let past failures hold you back from enjoying a happy life. You have nothing to lose but a heavy burden, but you have a lot to gain. The key to moving forward is to forgive yourself and those who hurt you. Stay in the now and affirm the good that has been a result of a bad situation. Love yourself more than you do. The same promise Jacob gave his son Joseph on his death bed, God gives us. He will be with us in the person of His son Jesus Christ.

No matter what comes up against you, do not weaken, stand against the darkness. That is another way back to life. The words alone, lonely and abandonment all contained the word 'One' when we believe we stand by ourselves to face life's difficulties, just one person against the world, we will often feel alone, lonely and abandon. (Psalms13:1-2). The God who deliver BB from the pit of Hell and who turn her darkness into light will do the same for you.

There were times when BB felt exhausted and felt like quitting. There were times when she felt like resigning from this side of life but then these thoughts of encouragement came to her mind, Look up and pray! Pray all night long and expressed the feelings that you think God had forgotten and rejected. He wants you to tell Him everything and be honest about your feelings. He would not criticize you. Look forward and think about the good that might come out of your situation. His ways are perfect. Then take that time to look at your circumstances with eyes of faith. Ask the Lord to help you see your problems and not be discouraged and weary, but to see Him in the midst of them. Your problems are opportunities to discover Gods solutions.

Remind yourself daily that God is God of great wonders and can be trusted. Pour out your heart to Him and as you read each promise say to yourself, 'this promise is mine'. If, you are still experiencing feelings of doubt and discouragement pour out your hurt and ask Him to quash the enemy who so mercilessly attacked you. Sing, God loves when you sing to Him and when He hears you, He leans over with a smile and cheerfully listens and say, sing on my child, I hear you and I am here to your rescue and will deliver you and make your road easier and smoother.

Another thing God wants from you is patience it takes away worry. He knows your need better than you do. His purpose in waiting is to bring glory out of it all. Instead of having the delaying time of letting go, ask God for courage, patience and for His love. Then surrender unto Him that is when His work begins.

When you surrender, there will come gifts of hope and clarity. That broken heart and shattered spirit willsense that healing is taking place. He will pick up the broken pieces of your life and mend them back together.

Do not quit when your problems seemed beyond you. Be strong in mind and spirit. Leave the outcome to God. He promised not to make it too difficult for victory is already yours. Do not worry about yesterday and tomorrow, rest today. Trust in the Lord and he will take care of your past, present and your future. He will enable you to change lanes on your express way, to enable you to fulfill your divine promise to get to the kingdom which involves determination, decisions and your destiny. For God is your stronghold in times of troubles and He promises you victory in the midst of your struggles that will empower you to hold on until your deliverance comes.

Readers, God loves you. He does not get tired of hearing about our troubles. He loves us this much that He gave His only begotten son to die for us and those who believe in Him shall not perish but have eternal life. Jesus laid down His life for us so that we could experience his absolute best here on earth. A man who knew no sin became sin for us.

When we struggle with the same problems over and over, God allows them so we can come to Him for help and to make us humble, to draw us away from the ills of this world and to drive us back to Him. He wants us to hasten our prayers and to become more and more dependent on Him, to experience more of His faithfulness and to submit to His way and to His will to that He has purposed for our life. If He seemed far away, just sincerely keep on searching for Him. His Word says 'if you keep on looking, you will find him. The same way He has helped people in the past, He will help you.

My friends, do not be surprised at the terrible troubles which now come to test you. Do not think that something strange is happening to you. But be happy that you are sharing in Christs' sufferings so that you will be happy and full of joy when He comes again in glory. Finally, after reading this and you are not a Christian and is now willing and ready to accept Jesus into your life as your personal Lord and Savior now is the time to do so. 2 Corinthians 6:2 says 'Now is the accepted time, behold, now is the day of salvation Romans 10:9,10 and 13 say: If you confess with your mouth the Lord Jesus and believe in your heart that God has raised him from the dead, you will be Saved. For with the heart one believes unto righteousness and with the mouth confession is made unto salvation. Whosoever calls on the name of the Lord shall be saved. 2 Corinthians 5:17 further states: 'Therefore if any man be in Christ he is a new creation; old things have passed away; behold, all things have become new.

If you believed these confirmations, say the following sinner's prayer out loud.

'Heavenly father, I come to you, admitting that I am a sinner. Right now, I choose to turn away from sin, and the ways of this world and ask You to cleanse me of all unrighteousness. I believe that Jesus died for me and rose again from the dead, so that I might be forgiven of my sins, and made righteous through faith in God. I call upon the name of Jesus Christ to be the Lord and Savior of my life. Jesus right now, I choose to follow You and make you my Lord and Savior. Make me Your child. Fill me with the power of Your Holy Spirit free from sin, bondage, the ills of this world, hurt, pain and from abuse. I declare this right now by faith. In the name that is above all names, the name of Your Son Jesus Christ' Amen.

Saints, this is what God told us. He has given us eternal life, and this life is in His Son. Whoever has the Son has life, but whoever does not have the Son of God does not have life. I write this letter to you who believe in the Son of God so you will know you have eternal life. (1John 5:11-13)

These words BB leaves with you. She implores you to 'Read God's Word daily!' Because His Word is sharper than any two-edge sword. Pray without ceasing! Prayer is a very powerful tool. If you do these things, you will see great and mighty miracles taking place in your life.

BB's Prayer of thanksgiving

Now God, in the name of Your son Jesus, BB personally thank You for giving her the inspiration, wisdom knowledge and understanding for writing this book to both hurting men and women in the world today. Dear God, as they read the pages, may its content bring them healing, comfort and restoration. May it free them from all the destructive forces that the devil tries to build around them. Be their protector and their avenger all the days of their lives. Bless them as she continues to intercede on their behalf. With the authority given her in Christ Jesus she sends back every wicked spirit that has been assigned against them and that every hurt and abusive relationship be cancelled in the name of Jesus Christ of Nazareth. Lord, thank you for placing Your wonderful, powerful, protective peace in BB's life. She is eternally grateful to You for positioning her to take on such a task. Thank You, Thank You, Thank You, Amen, Amen and Amen.

READ AND BE BLESSED!

REFERENCES – TEXT CREDITS

The King James Version and New Living Translation – TBN Parallel Version.

The African-American Devotional Bible Kings James Version – Zondervan

The Divine facts you need -Divorce - information (Internet)

Life Application Study Bible - Tyndale

Life's Daily Prayer Book - Elin Hill

God's in the small stuff - Bruce Bickel and Stan Jantz

God's Words of life – NIV – Women's Devotional Bible – Zondervan

Webster's 11 New Riverside Dictionary - Brighton Mifflin

God's Promises for every day - New Century Version.

Printed in the United States
By Bookmasters